Hanging in There

by John Dickson

FOR MUM

Other publications by John Dickson:
A Hell of a Life
A Sneaking Suspicion
If I were God, I'd end all the pain
Simply Christianity: Beyond Religion

John can be contacted in cyber-space care of:
jdickson@matthiasmedia.com.au

Hanging in There © Matthias Media
First Printed 1991, 2nd Edition 1997
St Matthias Press Ltd ACN 067 558 365

PO Box 225, Kingsford NSW 2032, Australia
Telephone (02) 9663 1478 Facsimile (02) 9663 3265
International +61-2-9663 1478 Facsimile +61-2-9663 3265
E-mail: sales@matthiasmedia.com.au
Website: www.matthiasmedia.com.au

Unless otherwise indicated, Scripture verses taken from:
the HOLY BIBLE, NEW INTERNATIONAL VERSION.
Copyright ©1973, 1978, 1984 International Bible Society.
Used by permission of Zondervan Bible Publishers.

All illustrations by David Cornish
Design and typesetting by Joy Lankshear Design Pty Ltd
Printed in Australia

CONTENTS

WHY THIS BOOK?

In this book I've tried to set down in a modern way what I think are the most relevant issues for people who want to live the Christian life.

Each of the chapters deals with a topic I've spoken on many times, whether privately to a school student or on stage to a audience. Touring with the band *In The Silence,* and by myself, has convinced me that there is a need for a book like this–a basic book about Christianity for young people (say, 25 and under). You might be:

- new to the Christian faith;
- fairly interested in it;
- a 'longer serving' Christian who needs a bit of encouragement.

Whichever way, this book might be for you.

Each chapter is self-contained and doesn't necessarily lead into the next, so you can read any chapter at any time. However, there is a logical flow, so you might find it easier to read the chapters in order.

If you own a Bible, it's probably a good idea to keep it handy as you go through this book. All the Bible verses I've quoted are taken from the New International Version (unless otherwise specified) so if you have that version you'll be right. If not, don't worry–you'll still be able to follow with other versions. If you're not sure how to look up Bible references (for example, 2 Cor 5:17), have a quick look at page 32 in chapter 4 before you get started.

You will notice that at the end of most chapters there are a few Bible verses listed. If you're interested in knowing more about the topic dealt with in a particular chapter these will help you to investigate it further.

I certainly don't expect this book to make me rich and famous. I simply hope that it will be a help to those keen on hanging in there with God.

John Dickson

CLEARING THE CONFUSION
The 'how' and 'what' of a Christian

WHEN MY MATES and I first picked up our instruments to form a band, it was a case of "OK, who wants to play what?" Ben wanted to play guitar so he went up to the local music shop, found a black one (they sound better) and bought it. Angus (who got 5% in music at school) took to the bass and, because I was the biggest poser of the lot, I became the lead singer. Jacques, who had never played an instrument either, joined us on the drums some time later.

At first we wanted to play songs from 'real bands' but we soon discovered that there's only so much you can do when you only know two or three chords. So we started to write our own songs in an attempt to explain our faith in a way that is easily understood.

From those laughable beginnings we ended up touring full-time around Australia and overseas playing in schools, prisons and universities. They were the most exciting and challenging years of my life.

I remember one of our high school seminars in particular. After more than an hour of songs and talks, we invited people to make comments or ask questions. Straight away, a hand shot up. "You've told us how and why you guys became Christians but how exactly do *I* become a Christian?"

The question is a good one. How do we become God's friend? How can we know for sure that God has a place for us in his family? "How exactly do I become a Christian?" This first chapter is dedicated to answering this all important question.

The news about Jesus Christ has been a major talking point throughout history. It has transformed the lives of kings and peasants, rich and poor, brainiacs and thick heads, bikers and yuppies, dags and cools, kids and olds. The list goes on.

The news is all about the solution to a huge problem.

WHAT PROBLEM?

I think most of us live in a society madly trying to convince us that everything is cool. All you need is Coke, Reeboks, a stereo, a girl or guy and the occasional pass in exams or job promotion and you're set. But everything is not cool, especially if what Jesus said is true.

The basic problem is that we have all ignored the Creator of the universe and rebelled against him. We don't want him telling us what to do, and so we either don't take any notice of him or just outright disobey him. As a result, we are guilty before him and cut off from having a friendship with him.

Now that's pretty bad news, I know, but there is no nice way to say it. I mean, how do you pleasantly explain to a surfer that there's a three

metre White Pointer coming his way?

Being the owner of the world, God has a right to tell us what to do. He's the boss. And in our own different ways, we all resist him and his authority. We don't obey his guidelines and we don't thank him and respect him for who he is. The consequences of this need to be looked at head on.

Jesus explained that one day everyone will be judged for what they have or haven't done.

There is a judge for the one who rejects me and does not accept my words; that very word which I spoke will condemn him at the last day.

John 12:48

Some people say, "Oh, that's scare tactics". But again, if you warn a surfer about that three metre shark, is that scare tactics?

I want to stop here and make one thing very clear: God does not get a kick out of punishing people. God is loving. No matter who you are or what you've done, he cares for you heaps. God is not a big, bearded grandfather figure sitting on a cloud waiting to hit us over the head with a stick every time we disobey him. A loving parent will still punish their child for doing something wrong. Likewise, justice is part of God's personality–he loves us enough to care about what we do and to punish us for doing wrong.

People often argue, "But what about the good things I've done?" Yes, God sees the good things, but he doesn't have a set of cosmic scales designed to weigh up the good against the bad.

If someone commits a crime in our society, they can't say to the judge in a courtroom, "But Your Honour, just before I mugged that kid I helped an old lady across the road". The judge may think to himself, "Yes, that's nice", but he would not let the crime go unpunished. To do so would betray his position as a judge. Likewise, God sees our disobedience and will act accordingly.

As well as being guilty, the Bible also describes us as being cut off from the life God wants for us. In the very beginning, God wanted us to have a life filled with his life and friendship. When we disobeyed him, all this went wrong.

An illustration may help explain what I mean. Imagine cutting a single rose off a rose bush and sticking it in a glass of water. It looks good and smells good (if you're into that sort of thing) but really it's dying. It's cut off from its source of life. You could feed it Coke, give it a pair of Reeboks, and play it U2 day and night, but in a few days you'd see that it really was lifeless.

Just like the rose, people are cut off from the 'life source'. God is the source of real life but because of our disobedience we can't have any of it. I've met people who argue, "But I feel great about my life". Sure, but so does the rose in a glass of water...for a while. God's book says that we are all "dead in...(our) transgressions" (Eph 2:1). That's not a good situation to be in.

Fortunately, the Christian message does not end on this depressing tone. God has a solution that blows away the problem.

THE SOLUTION

Less than 50 generations ago, the man Jesus lived, taught, healed and generally caused a huge stir. In that part of the world (the Middle East), he was known by just about everyone. He was hated by some and loved by others. At about the age of 33 he was arrested and put on trial before the officials of the day. He was accused of insulting God because he claimed things about himself which only God could claim. This was a very serious crime in those days.

After being beaten and whipped, he was nailed to a cross and died. Three days later, he came back to life and appeared to heaps of people, showing that he was in fact the Son of God. The big question is, why did the all-powerful, all-knowing Designer of the universe give up his position of power, safety and respect to become a man and die at the hands of his own creation?

The answer is simple–he loves us! Not with a weak, soppy kind of love, but a love that is passionate and strong.

By dying on that cross, Jesus Christ took the penalty you and I deserve. Instead of you and me being condemned, he was condemned. Instead of you and me being cut off from God, he was cut off. He was innocent but he took the blame for you and me.

This is how the prophet Isaiah describes it:

Surely he took up our infirmities and carried our sorrows, yet we considered him stricken by God, smitten by him, and afflicted. But he was pierced for our transgressions, he was crushed for our iniquities; the punishment that brought us peace was upon him, and by his wounds we are healed. We all, like sheep, have gone astray, each of us has turned to his own way; and the LORD has laid on him the iniquity of us all.

Isaiah 53:4-6

At age 15, this fact had an impact on my life that could never be reversed. I was obsessed with martial arts and thought it was cool to be cruel to others. I stole for a hobby and lived by the rule 'if it feels good, do it'. I deserved a penalty but Jesus paid my fine. It was as if he became the 15 year-old jerk and took my place.

So then, God's solution cancels out our problem. Our rebellion resulted in us becoming guilty but Jesus' death and resurrection provides complete and undeserved forgiveness. In fact, a Christian is not only forgiven, but God also considers them to be good, or 'righteous'.

The Bible reads:

God made him who had no sin to be sin for us, so that in him we might become the righteousness of God.   **2 Corinthians 5:21**

A big swap occurred. Jesus took our disobedience and its consequences, and we got his goodness and all its consequences. It's sort of like Mel Gibson coming to me and saying, "Hey, John, I'll take your face and you can have mine". It sounds too good to be true, doesn't it? But the loving, powerful God has done it.

In botanical science, there is a process known as 'grafting' which allows us to take a single rose stem and restore it back onto the branch from which it came. There it receives new life from its source. God has been doing a similar thing with people for centuries.

When someone becomes a Christian, they are instantly joined back to their life source–God. Once this happens, God opens up to them a whole new life, full of the things he originally intended for them. Things like love, purpose in life, and lots more. I'll elaborate on this in the following chapters.

A Christian is someone who has received the forgiveness and new life which God freely offers. This is God's huge solution to our problem.

OUR RESPONSE

I once met a Year 10 student who had understood the Christian message and agreed with it, but wanted to know how to respond to it in order to become a Christian herself.

My answer went something along the following lines.

It's a bit obvious I know, but before becoming a Christian you have to get your facts straight. Do you know that you're guilty before God and cut off from him? Do you believe that Jesus Christ died to take the blow that you and I deserve and then rose again?

Once you agree with the facts, God then wants you to trust him (in the Bible, you'll see the word 'faith' a lot; it usually means simply 'trust'). Imagine a young girl, stuck up a tree, whose mother comes to the rescue. She may agree in her head that her mum can hold her, but until she trusts her and lets go of the tree she will remain stuck.

Likewise, before you can become a Christian you not only need to know in your head that Christ died to take the world's punishment but also trust that he took your punishment so that *you* could be forgiven.

Some people only half trust God. They feel that they also need to try and do good things in order to make themselves worthy. Half their trust is in God; the other half is in their own 'goodness'. This is not what God wants. He is completely trustworthy. Christ's death is more than enough to bring us forgiveness and new life. Trust him!

Once you've trusted him, simply ask God to forgive you. It's like saying sorry to someone you've wronged, only a much bigger deal. Remember, he is ready, able and very keen to hear you. If you're not too sure about what to pray, there is an example at the end of the chapter.

In every day situations an apology usually means two things. Firstly, that we're sorry, and secondly, that we intend to stop whatever it is we're sorry for. It's the same in becoming a Christian. How can we ask God to forgive us unless we intend to turn from rebelling against him and begin putting him first?

When I became a Christian, I stopped stealing, hurting people and living for myself. I didn't become an angel overnight (just ask my mum, wife, friends, etc.) but my attitude certainly changed. I made it my aim to treat God as Boss. This didn't earn God's forgiveness but I really was sorry and I was thankful for everything he'd done.

Get the facts straight, then trust, ask and turn. This is how we step out of our problem and into God's wonderful solution. If you've never done that, perhaps you may want to tell God that you want his solution. The following prayer is not magical, but it may just help you express to God your desire to be a Christian.

> God, I know that I've done things that are wrong.
> I've ignored you and rebelled against you.
> I am truly sorry. Please forgive me.
> Thank you, Jesus, for taking my punishment on the cross.
> Thank you that you love me and will forgive me.
> I know you are alive and I want to obey you from now on.
> You're the boss. Thanks again. Amen

Check These Out

- ▶ Rom 6:23
- ▶ Rom 10:13
- ▶ 1 John 1:9
- ▶ Eph 2:8

RULE NO.1
God loves you heaps!

A FEW YEARS AGO a young couple were on their honeymoon at Coffs Harbour. They both loved scuba diving and decided to spend their first weeks of marriage diving at Julian Rocks only a few kilometres off the main beach at Byron Bay. I remember watching the television and seeing the new wife in tears. The diving trip had gone horribly wrong–her husband had been attacked and killed by a shark. In tears she explained what happened.

All I can remember is turning around and seeing a White Pointer with its jaws open coming for me and I thought it was all over. Just before the shark took me, my husband pushed me out of the way and placed himself between me and the shark. The shark attacked him and now he is gone forever.

It's a moving story, isn't it? You can be sure that incident will stay with the woman for the rest of her life, not only because of the trauma of the event but also because of the powerful display of love her husband had shown. She will never, ever, be able to doubt just how much he loved her. Nothing speaks louder about love than giving up a life for someone else.

This chapter is about that kind of love. In fact, it's about a love that is even more extreme than this example. It's about God's love.

This may seem like a strange subject to put so early in the book, but there is a real reason for doing this. As I meet more and more Christians in my travels I am realising that many of God's people get caught in a trap where they lose sight of God's love for them. They end up serving God out of fear and stress rather than excitement and thankfulness. This, of course, can lead to guilt and depression.

However, if you can learn the golden rule of Christianity early on in your adventure with God, you will enjoy a firm foundation for the rest of your life. The truth is simple–as a Christian, you are and will always remain the focus of God's deep favour and love. Many Christians have hassles because they misunderstand the reality of how God views them. Learn this reality and you will avoid many of these unnecessary hang-ups.

The Bible has heaps to say about God's love for us. In fact, it is one of the main themes throughout the whole book. Here are some of the major thoughts concerning God's love found there.

PLANNED LOVE

When that man put himself between the shark and his wife, it was a split-second decision. It was a reflex action, full of fear and adrenalin. God's love is every bit as passionate, but it is no reflex action. God's decision to love you was not a split-second one, made in the heat of a dangerous moment. It was a decision made before you were even born. Even Jesus' death for you was not a last minute thing. That, too, was decided way back in eternity. God's love for you is well planned.

UNDESERVED LOVE

There is another difference between the love the husband showed and the love God has shown. Quite simply, the wife was an innocent tourist. It was quite appropriate that someone (especially her husband) should try and rescue her. But we are not innocent, and we certainly don't deserve God's rescue. Despite this, however, God has gone beyond the call of duty. It's amazing to think that God knows all of our selfishness, pride, violence, lying, etc, and yet he still gave up his son to die for us. The Bible says:

You see, at just the right time, when we were still powerless, Christ died for the ungodly. Very rarely will anyone die for a righteous man, though for a good man someone might possibly dare to die. But God demonstrates his own love for us in this: while we were still sinners, Christ died for us.

Romans 5:6-8

SELF-SACRIFICING LOVE

I don't know about you but sometimes I find it near impossible to give things up for other people. When I used to live at home one of the hardest things for me to give up was my free time (giving up half an hour to mow the lawn would almost kill me!). But thank God, God does not have my problem. It's second nature for him to give up things for us. It's just the kind of person he is. It's weird to realise that God, who is Boss of everything, could love us so much that he would make some serious sacrifices for us. When Christ became a man, he left all his glory, honour and power behind. On top of that, he gave up his life in a terrible death so that we could become his friends. He put us first. He didn't need us. He could have just left us guilty, but he didn't. He loved us.

ACCEPTING LOVE

When a Christian does something wrong, they sometimes think, "Oh no, God's not going to love me now" and so they feel scared to go to him for forgiveness. This is one of the big mistakes in the Christian life.

But the Bible says:

My dear children, I write this to you so that you will not sin. But if anybody does sin, we have one who speaks to the Father in our defence-Jesus Christ, the Righteous One. He is the sacrifice that takes away the punishment our sins deserve. But not only the punishment our sins deserve-also the sins of the whole world.
1 John 2:1-2

This means that even if we dishonour God, he doesn't 'write us off'. Of course, this doesn't mean that we have a licence to do whatever we want. Sin is still wrong. But remember, as Christians, we can go to God without fear and obtain his instant forgiveness.

One of the best examples of this 'accepting love' is found in the New Testament (the second part of the Bible). We are told about how Peter the apostle betrayed Jesus and even denied knowing him. Shortly after this, Jesus was killed. Imagine how guilty Peter would have felt. He had been close friends with Jesus for three years and yet, in one moment of fear, he threw it all away. After Jesus rose, three days later, he appeared to his disciples a number of times. One of those times was down at the beach where he took Peter aside to have a private chat. I'm sure Peter expected to get in big trouble, and perhaps even get put back a few spaces. Instead, far from being put backwards, Peter was asked by the Lord to be a leader of the Christians. The Lord knew that Peter was sorry and didn't hold his betrayal against him. This is how God deals with all his children.

NEVER-ENDING LOVE

God's love doesn't stop here either. In fact, that's my point–it doesn't stop! Regardless of your circumstances, you are never beyond the reach of God's love. Somewhere way back in eternity, God set his love upon you and it will continue, unchanged, all the way into a never-ending future. Even when we feel like dirt, the Bible is still clear that nothing will ever be able to separate us from God's love:

> For I am convinced that neither death nor life, neither angels nor demons, neither the present nor the future, nor any powers, neither height nor depth, nor anything else in all creation, will be able to separate us from the love of God that is in Christ Jesus our Lord.   **Romans 8:38-39**

HOW TO KNOW GOD'S LOVE

As I've already said, if you can grasp this truth about God's love early in your Christian life, you will avoid many of the hang-ups some Christians experience.

A good friend of mine has given up her faith in Christ because she never really understood how much God loved and cared for her. She constantly felt guilty and under pressure to please him. This led to lots of stress. She said she felt chained rather than free. This will quickly damage anyone's faith.

But it doesn't have to be that way. In fact, it should never happen that way. We can know God's love, and this love will change us forever.

The question then arises, "How do I get to feel God's love?" Many people have a problem with this, particularly if they've been deeply hurt by some past experience. Sometimes I meet teenagers who have been let down by people they loved and who loved them. This often leaves a reluctance to accept that someone loves them, particularly God. Here are a couple of tips about knowing God's love.

- Don't worry about trying to 'feel' God's love. It's not a 'warm fuzzy' that floats through the air waiting to touch someone. Start with believing it. Good news makes us happy when we believe it, not before.
- The way to know anybody's love is to trust what they say and look at what they do. If someone tells you they love you and they also act like it, you can be pretty sure they do. God meets this criteria, don't you think?
- The best way to know God's love is to turn to the Bible and read for yourself what he has said and what he has done. The supreme demonstration of this love for us is the way he sacrificed his Son for our sins. By understanding what Jesus has done on the cross, we see a God whose love is real and gutsy. Spend some time thinking about it, put your trust in it, and once it grabs you, you'll never be the same again.

Here are some Bible passages about God's amazing love for you. Look them up, read them, think about them and ask him to help you understand them. As you do, I'm sure that you will grow more and more in your confidence in this wonderful God of ours.

Check These Out

▶ **Psalm 103**   ▶ **Psalm 118:1**

▶ **Psalm 145:8-9**   ▶ **Romans 5:1-11**

▶ **Ephesians 3:18-19**

GOD IN A BOOK
Making sense of the Bible

CHINESE READ IT, Russians read it, Romanians read it, Tibetans read it, Africans read it, Lithuanians read it, Aborigines read it, Lebanese read it, Greeks read it, Germans read it, the Welsh read it...Do you get the picture? The Bible–by far the biggest selling book of all history.

Apart from being the number one best-seller of all time, the Bible is probably also number one for being 'the most misunderstood book'.

To some, it's a nice ornament to be placed neatly on the shelf. To others, it's a sentimental thing to be kept beside the bed but never actually read. Still others see it as a book to be scared of. "Help! Bible bashers!" is a cry some people make when introduced to Christians.

Just about everyone has an opinion concerning this best-seller: "It's a pack of lies"; "It's so irrelevant"; "It's been changed through time"; "It's just a good fairytale". It's interesting to meet people who hold these opinions. I'm often amused to see them blush when I ask if they've actually read this 'irrelevant fairytale' for themselves.

WHAT IS IT?

The Bible is the Word of God. By this I mean that the Creator of the universe chose to communicate with us in a lasting way in the pages of a book. This is a brilliant idea if you ask me. It means that our knowledge and relationship with God is based on something solid. It's not like we need to have mystical/magical feelings to get in touch with God. Nor do we have to go somewhere spiritual–a mountainside or church for example–to hear his voice. We get in touch with God and hear his voice in a very simple, practical and unconfusing way–by reading words on a page!

If you bought the latest 300 watt stereo system with a multi-CD player, dual cassette, turntable and a 31-band graphic equalizer, all programmable by remote control, you'd probably take notice of the instructions before you tried it out. Everything we need to know about God's character and plan for us is found in the Bible. It is the ultimate Manufacturer's Instructions. And yet it is more than just an instruction manual. As you read it, you will find it to be a very warm, down-to-earth account of God's relationship with human beings throughout history.

Across the pages of God's book are accounts of war and peace, violence and compassion, assassination and resurrection, Satan and God, past events and even future events. Not bad for such an 'old book'.

The Bible is divided into two main sections: the Old Testament and the New Testament. (The word 'testament' means a 'covenant' or 'contract'.) In the Old Testament, there are 39 separate books and in the New there are 27. It's like a small library, except you don't have to go searching too far to get what you want. Each new title in the Bible is counted as a different book. For example, 'Genesis' is one book and 'Exodus' is another. There are all kinds of different books too–there's history, poetry, song lyrics, biography, wise sayings, adventure stories–but all of it is God's Word and all of it can be trusted.

The Old Testament is basically an account of God's dealings with one particular nation called Israel. God chose Israel to be the vehicle of his blessing and favour to the rest of the world. We read of wars and great heroes, of God's love and his judgement. Most importantly, the Old Testament is full of predictions and preparations for the time when Jesus would come and bring people from every part of the world back into friendship with the Almighty God.

To understand the difference between the Old and New Testaments, imagine looking at a man and his shadow. The shadow reveals the outline and certain features of the man but not in much detail. This is similar to the Old Testament explanation of God's plan for the world, where all we know is that God will bless the entire world through one of Israel's leaders (the coming Messiah or Christ).

The New Testament, however, brings that plan into sharp focus. It's like turning from the shadow to look at the man face to face. That man, of course, is Jesus Christ. He is the great leader who opens the way for the whole world to experience God's love and life.

Of the 27 books in the New Testament, the first four are accounts of Jesus' life, death and resurrection written by people who were either there when the events took place, or were at least very close in time to the events. These books are known as the Gospels. The fifth book is also sort of a history/biography. It's called Acts and it describes the first few decades after Jesus returned to Heaven, and how the first disciples got the gospel message rolling around the world.

When I say the word 'history', don't think I mean boring facts and figures. These first five books of the New Testament are the most exciting history books you'll come across because they tell of the most important person that ever set foot on the planet.

The rest of the New Testament is a collection of letters written by Christian leaders. These letters were sent to other Christian leaders and to the early churches as a way of encouraging and teaching them. The weird names of the letters simply indicate the places where each letter was sent, the name of the sender, or the name of the receiver. For example, 'Ephesians' was sent to a place called Ephesus. 'James' was written by a bloke called James, and 'Timothy' was written to a bloke called Timothy. It's all pretty basic when you get into it.

WHO WROTE IT AND WHEN?

The Bible is God's word to mankind but he used many different people to write it down. Over a period of 1600 years, kings, shepherds, fishermen, priests, a doctor, a tax collector and others were inspired by God with thoughts and words which they wrote down. The last book of the New Testament was written by about 90 AD, leaving Christians ever since with the complete unchanging words of the unchanging Creator. I'm sorry if this sounds like an ad for Coke or something, but as you can probably work out, I love God's book, and want you to get into it for yourself.

HAS IT CHANGED?

Sometimes people say things like: "The Bible has been passed down from generation to generation. It has been translated from one language to another, to another, and so has lost its original meaning".

This, in fact, is not true. Most of the English Bibles available today are direct translations of the original languages in which it was written (Hebrew, Aramaic and Greek). Although hand-copying occurred many times (no printers back then), the skill of the copiers (or scribes) ensured the accuracy of these special writings. The following true story may help to show just how reliable our modern Bible is.

In the spring of 1947, an Arab shepherd boy, having lost one of his goats, set out on a search among the valleys of the Judean wilderness near the Dead Sea. Casually throwing a rock into a hillside cave, he heard the sound of breaking pottery. He climbed in to investigate, and found pottery jars containing leather scrolls wrapped in linen. These leather scrolls turned out to be the most significant document discovery of modern archaeology. Among them was a scroll containing the Old Testament book of Isaiah. The scroll was dated at about 2000 years old.

When this ancient copy of this part of the Bible was compared to the modern version, the accuracy was astonishing. What we read now, is in fact, what was written thousands of years ago.

WHAT ABOUT DIFFERENT VERSIONS?

Choosing a particular version of the Bible can be quite confusing. Popular ones include the Revised Standard Version, New International Version, Contemporary English Version, King James, New King James, New American Standard, Good News, The Living Bible and heaps, heaps more.

Now, don't worry. They are all the same Bible and all say the same thing–they simply differ in the English used. This makes some easier to read than others. I suggest you read the New International Version. It is very easy to read as well as being an accurate translation.

Here's an example of a verse in different translations. The verse is John 5:24.

New International Version:
I tell you the truth, whoever hears my word and believes him who sent me has eternal life and will not be condemned; he has crossed over from death to life.

Good News Bible:
I am telling you the truth: whoever hears my words and believes in him who sent me has eternal life. He will not be judged but has already passed from death to life.

New American Standard Bible:
Truly, truly, I say to you, he who hears my word and believes him who sent me, has eternal life, and does not come into judgement, but has passed out of death into life.

King James Version:
Verily, verily, I say unto you, he that heareth my word and believeth on him that sent me, hath everlasting life, and shall not come into condenmation; but is passed from death unto life.

WHY READ IT?

In some countries, like China, it is still very difficult to get your hands on God's book. You can't just rock down to your local bookstore and say, "Hey! Comrade! Can I have a couple of Bibles please?" It is only recently that Bibles have been printed in China. Before that, they were smuggled in through customs from 'free' countries, and then distributed to underground Chinese church leaders. I know people who have done it. Many churches in these areas are lucky to have one Bible for the whole congregation. They are crying out to read God's Word but it just isn't available.

In our country, things are very different. Instead of crying out for Bibles, we sit them on the shelf to collect dust. Some Christians find it hard to get stuck into the Bible. They see it as a kind of 'task' that has to be done in order to make you spiritually healthy, like a kind of spiritual brussel sprout–hard to swallow but good for you. As a result, the Bible loses its excitement for these Christians.

This is very sad. It is not at all what God wants. His word is 'alive', and he wants that life to get hold of us:

For the word of God is living and active. Sharper than any double-edged sword, it penetrates even to dividing soul and spirit, joints and marrow; it judges the thoughts and attitudes of the heart. Hebrews 4:12

Someone once said that the Bible is the only book where the author himself is present every time you read it. You can be sure that as you read his book, the Author will guide you, teach you, warn you, and make you strong in your faith. That's a pretty good reason to get into it.

It's also a good reason to read the next chapter.

Check These Out

▶ **2 Tim 3:16-17**
▶ **Prov 30:5**

FINDING GOD IN THE BOOK
Getting the most out of the Bible

FOR THE FIRST FEW MONTHS of my Christian life, I had questions coming out of my ears. Luckily, I knew some older Christians at church who pointed me to the Bible for answers. I soon learnt that everything I needed to know about living as God's child could be found in his book.

In this chapter, I want to offer some help as to how to get the most out of the Bible because simply diving straight in doesn't always work out. For example, you may turn to Numbers 26:12 and read:

The descendants of Simeon by their class were:

through Nemuel, the Nemuelite clan;

through Jamin, the Jaminite clan;

through Jakin, the Jakinite clan;

through Zerah, the Zerahite clan;

through Shaul, the Shaulite clan.

These were the clans of Simeon; there were 22,200 men.

Now, all this would have been important to old Simeon, but I'm sure there are easier passages in the Bible for you and me, especially to start with.

I want to make a few suggestions, based on the way I first started to study God's book. Hopefully, this will be of some help as you begin reading his word for yourself.

HOW TO LOOK UP A BIBLE REFERENCE

If you are new to the idea of reading the Bible then there's something you need to get the hang of–finding Bible verses.

The people who wrote the Bible are not the ones who put all the reference numbers in. In fact, they didn't even name their own books. These things were done centuries later. Some pretty smart people got together and invented a way to make finding certain Bible quotes a whole lot easier. Imagine trying to find 2 Cor 5:17 by the following instructions: "Read the third sentence in the twenty-fourth paragraph of the second letter Paul wrote to the Church at Corinth."

In our example (2 Cor 5:17) the first part, '2 Cor', refers to the name of the book–i.e., the second book of Corinthians ('Cor' for short). The next number ('5') always refers to the chapter in which to look. (Chapter numbers are marked in the Bible by large type.) The last number ('17') directs you to the actual verse you are looking for. If more than one verse is referenced, for example, 2 Cor 5:17-21, it simply means to read verses 17 to 21 (inclusive). Verses are marked in your Bible in small type, tucked in amongst the writing.

If there is only one book with a particular title, then only the name of the book will be given. For example, the book of Romans is the only one with this name and so will not read '1 Romans'. The only exception to this rule is the book of 'John' in the New Testament. This is the title given to the book John the Apostle wrote about Jesus' life. However, John also wrote three letters separate to his Gospel. These are given the names, 1 John, 2 John and 3 John, and are found towards the back of the Bible.

Remember, if you have any troubles finding where a book is placed in the Bible, use the index. That's what it's there for. Don't ever feel embarrassed that you don't know your way around this little 'library of books'–it takes a while to learn.

WHERE TO LEARN

Looking at Simeon in the book of Numbers is probably not the best place to begin your reading of the Bible. I suggest finding a book in the New Testament, perhaps the second one, the Gospel of Mark. The first four books in the New Testament are pretty similar in that they all tell us about Jesus' life and teachings. I prefer the Gospel of Mark because it is short and punchy. If you've already read this 'Gospel', then you might like to try Acts or 1 John.

Once you've chosen a book, it's best to gradually read it all the way through so you catch the flow of what it's saying.

For a while I used to open the Bible at random and expect to read something amazing every time. God might occasionally use this 'open and read' method, but I'm sure he'd rather us be a bit more logical in our reading. After all, nearly every book in the Bible was written with the intention of being read out loud (to a meeting of God's people), from start to finish, all in one hit.

HOW TO START

1. PRAY

Before we read God's word, it's always good to ask for his help to understand the passage. Remember, he wrote it, and only he can fully explain it to our little brains. (If the idea of prayer is a bit foreign to you, don't panic, we'll cover that in the next chapter.)

2. READ

You may only want to read a page at a time or maybe you'll want to read heaps more. Either way is cool. God is pleased with both. Usually a combination of both is best–you can get the overall picture of what's being said by reading a big slab and then zoom in on the details by looking at a few verses at a time. It's a bit like breakfast. Whether you pig out like me or eat moderately like my wife, Buff, it's still important that you eat something–and preferably most days of the week!

3. THINK

This may sound obvious but once you've read a passage it's good to sit back and think about it for a few minutes. Often things become a lot clearer and more relevant if we give ourselves time to think.

Thinking about how you can apply what you've read is probably the most important part of reading the Bible. For example, I may read John 13:34-35, where Jesus says:

A new command I give you: love one another. As I have loved you, so you must love one another. By this all men will know that you are my disciples, if you love one another.

After reading this passage I should think of people in my daily situation and how I can show them love in a more practical way. I should ask myself: "How did Jesus show his love to others?" and then try to do the same.

4. WRITE IT DOWN

I've found it very helpful, over the years, to write down what I learn. After I've prayed, read and thought, I've then gone to my folder or note book and recorded it.

Keeping this kind of written record is good for two reasons. Firstly, it helps get your thoughts clear; and secondly, it's great to look back on and recall what God has taught you over the months and years.

Here's a copy of one of my first Bible studies using this method. The Bible passage I chose was 1 Peter 4:8-10.

Above all, love each other deeply, because love covers over a multitude of sins. Offer hospitality to one another without grumbling. Each one should use whatever gift he has received to serve others, faithfully administering God's grace in its various forms.

In my note book I wrote:

Saturday, 5th November Sat. 1 Peter 4:7-11.

Love wipes clean many sins. Each God-given gift must be used for the glory of God, not for yourself.

Special message: This shows that whatever is mine must be everyone else's to use for good. I must be willing to give my possessions and skills to everyone to use for good, without complaining.

I would write down the date, where the passage came from, what it basically talked about and then how it applied to me. I should also add that it is a good idea to end your reading of the Bible by praying that God would help you to put into practice what you got out of it.

The method I have described is only one way of studying the Bible. It worked for me for ages, but is not necessarily the best way. Hopefully it will help as a guide to start with, but I'm sure that as you continue, you will begin reading God's word in the way that is best for you.

The important thing to remember is that it is not magical or mysterious. Reading the Bible is not much different from reading the paper: you read it, see what it's saying, and then decide how it is relevant to you. Like a newspaper, most of it is pretty straightforward. Only occasionally are there very tricky bits that you might need help with. But unlike a newspaper, the Bible isn't out of date the next day—it tells us things that never change, like who God is, who we are and how we can get on with him.

My prayer is that as you read and understand his word, God will change you and show you why his book is history's all-time best-seller.

Check These Out

- ▶ **Psalm 19:8**
- ▶ **Psalm 119:11**
- ▶ **Eph 6:17**
- ▶ **Rom 15:4**

"UM . . . GOD?"

About prayer

Our Father, who art in heaven,
hallowed be thy Name,
thy kingdom come,
thy will be done
on earth as it is in heaven.
Give us this day our daily bread.
And forgive us our trespasses
as we forgive those who trespass against us.
And lead us not into temptation,
but deliver us from evil.
For thine is the kingdom,
the power and the glory
for ever and ever. Amen.

Before I was a Christian, I occasionally said this 'Lord's Prayer' (usually when I was scared of the dark or feeling lonely). I'm not too sure how I picked it up, since I never went to Sunday School or church. I knew the words but I certainly had no idea what they meant.

What is God 'arting' in Heaven for? Why is he called 'hallowed'? And what on earth is a 'trespass'?

I had missed the whole point of prayer. I saw it as a kind of magic spell. I figured that if I said a prayer at the right time (like before I fell asleep), it would give me a 'warm fuzzy' inside, or save me from God's anger, or perhaps assure me of that special Christmas present I wanted.

WHAT IS PRAYER?

After I became a Christian, things got a lot clearer. I found out that prayer is not a magic spell or a superstition, nor a spiritual exercise which religious people had to do (like push-ups for a footy player).

I discovered that prayer is simply talking to God. That may sound obvious but when you consider that we can freely and confidently talk to the Creator of the universe, that's a pretty amazing idea.

On tour in South Australia some time ago I stayed in a very large church building that looked more like the Sydney Entertainment Centre than a church. Throughout the building there were heaps of rooms, offices, stairs and corridors. To get to the Minister's office, you had to pass reception on the ground floor, walk up two flight of stairs to the administration area, ask politely to see the Minister, walk down the long corridor, knock on his office door and await his invitation to enter. However, when the Minister's son wants to see his dad, he simply runs past reception, up the stairs, ignores administration, confidently opens the office door and there finds his dad, always glad to see him.

This is a good picture of our special privilege as God's children. We can talk to him anywhere, any time, about anything, with confidence that he hears us. There are no barriers, reception lounges, administration areas or long corridors in between God and us.

This is the confidence we have in approaching God: that if we ask anything according to his will, he hears us. John 5:14

The amazing thing about being a Christian is that Jesus has removed the 'barrier' between us and God–our sin. Because of his death on the cross, where he took away our sin, prayer is suddenly possible. Because we've been forgiven, we can approach the mighty God of the Universe and talk to him as a father. In fact, that's precisely the point of the first line of that old 'Lord's Prayer' (it's called that because Jesus himself taught it)–it starts, "Our Father..." We are allowed to call God "father".

DIFFERENT ASPECTS OF PRAYER

Prayer is prayer, but it's probably helpful to think of talking to God in the following separate categories.

1. THANKS

It's always good to begin talking with God by thanking him for who he is, what he's done and what he's doing. Even the small things that happen in our life are worth thanking him for. The Bible says to "give thanks in all circumstances" (1 Thess 5:18). Even when things appear to be going badly, there are always plenty of things to thank God for–things we take for granted most of the time. And taking time out to thank him for all the good things we do have usually helps put the bad things in perspective.

2. CONFESSION

It's very important to spend a bit of time asking God to forgive you for anything you may have done wrong. There can sometimes be value in telling other Christians about your sin (they can pray for you) but it is not essential. God alone can forgive sin, so it's to him that we should go.

Remember, when as a Christian you disobey God it doesn't suddenly make you not a Christian. It doesn't change your relationship to him as your Father. We need not fear his rejection–so simply tell him what you've done, say sorry and decide to turn from doing it again.

If we confess our sins, he is faithful and just and will forgive us our sins and purify us from all unrighteousness. 1 John 1:9

Whatever you do, don't spend too much time trying to find something to confess. If you can't think of anything, just move on. You'll only depress yourself if you dwell too much on your failures. The Bible (and your conscience) will show you often enough when you've done the wrong thing.

3. FOR OTHERS

Some may disagree, but I think that the type of prayer that should take up most of our time talking to God is prayer for other people. The Bible has more to say about this type of prayer than any other.

God is loving, merciful and all-powerful. Knowing this should make us feel very confident about asking him to do things for others. There are people in need, Christians who are struggling and friends and relatives who don't know Jesus yet. God wants to answer your prayers for them.

If your dad was a billionaire, I'm sure you'd have no hassles asking him to use his money or influence to help one of your friends. God has a lot more influence and funds than a puny billionaire. I'm not saying that prayer is a slot machine for anything we want. Sometimes God doesn't answer our prayers in the way we want, for the same reason that a loving mum wouldn't buy her kid ten Mars bars, no matter how much he 'really' wanted them. God either answers, "yes", "no" or "wait a while". But remember, he will answer.

4. FOR YOURSELF

The easiest aspect of prayer is, of course, praying for ourselves. This is because we're usually far more interested in ourselves than others.

Jesus said, "...your Father knows what you need before you ask him". This is a pretty amazing promise when you think about it. Girl/boyfriends, exams, money, health, jobs–God knows and cares for all these aspects of your life. Feel free and confident about going to him for anything.

As long as we don't forget to pray for others, praying for ourselves can be a very exciting part of our life with God, particularly when we start to see real answers to our prayers.

There's one other thing. Whether you're praying for yourself or for others, look in the Bible for some clues about what to ask for. In the Bible, God tells us the kinds of things that are important to him, the things that are at the top of his list. These sorts of things should be the focus of our prayers. If we know what God wants (the religious word is his 'will') then we can pray with confidence, knowing that he will answer us.

There are other aspects of prayer, but these four points are the basis of all prayer and should help as guidelines.

WHEN TO PRAY

Some religions make it a rule to pray for strict amounts of time every day. Muslims, for example, must pray five times a day, every day at the same time. Fortunately, there is no such rule for God's children.

One of the most common problems among Christians is the feeling that they have to pray in order to be a 'good' Christian (whatever that means). Prayer becomes a task and a burden and they start to feel guilty when they don't do it enough.

This is all wrong! Do you talk to your family because you have to? Do you spend time with your friends because you have to? The answer is obviously no. When you love someone, it's only natural to talk to them. It's the same with God.

I know people who pray for an hour or two every day. They don't do it to earn a better motel room in God's kingdom, or to keep God from getting angry with them. They pray simply because they like talking to God, but this does not make them better Christians than someone who prays for ten minutes. To God, ten minutes of sincere prayer is better than an hour of disinterested mumbo-jumbo.

There is another extreme though. Some Christians spend two minutes a day with God and two hours in front of the TV and then wonder why God seems distant and 'The Simpsons' seems real.

I've found that setting aside time at the beginning of each day to pray is a very helpful practice. I'd suggest spending just a few minutes on each aspect of prayer each morning. If morning is not possible, evening is fine also. You can actually talk to the Lord any time, day or night. He never sleeps and is never too busy. In fact, he has more time for us than we do for him.

Walking, standing, kneeling, in the bedroom, on the toilet, in the shower–it makes no difference. God is with us all the time anyhow, so we might as well talk with him. My brother-in-law actually prays while he goes for his daily run. I know other people who stay in bed and pray. These things don't make much difference. When, where, how or what you pray is up to you. Just try and remember these last three important hints.

Firstly, God is loving and powerful which makes him willing and able to answer us. Don't feel that you have to use 'religious' words to make your prayers 'work'. Just speak to him as you speak to anyone that you love and respect.

Secondly, prayer can sometimes feel like you're talking to a brick wall. Feelings occasionally deceive us, so if we trust God instead of our feelings, brick walls won't hassle us.

Lastly, as I've already said, praying heaps (or not) does not make you a better (or worse) Christian. Don't let guilt bog you down–trust God. Concentrate on knowing and loving Jesus Christ. And ask God to help you. He won't let you down.

Check These Out

▶ **Matt 7:7-11**

▶ **Phil 4:6-7**

▶ **Rom 8:26**

CHURCH
What? Why? Which?

"I've decided that I'm going to be a Christian, but I've got a few questions, like: if you are a Christian, do you have to go to church...and stuff like that? Or can you just pray to God at home by yourself?"

THIS IS PART OF A LETTER I received from a student in Tamworth some time ago. The question is a good one. "Must I go to church?" If you're not used to going, it can be quite a weird experience. Before I was a Christian, I had only been to church once that I can remember. It was a funeral of someone I cared for a lot, so the experience wasn't a very happy one.

It didn't do much for my idea of churches at all. I sort of thought to myself, "Who would want to sit in a colourless building, on hard seats without cushions, singing 200-year-old songs for a whole hour?" Little did I know how stupid this attitude was.

Since age fifteen, when I began to follow Christ, I've been to many different churches. My travels have taken me to Anglican churches, Presbyterian churches, Baptist churches, Uniting, Brethren and Lutheran churches, AOG, CLC, CCC, COC churches and others. My view of churches has dramatically changed.

In this chapter I want to explain three things about churches, and hopefully settle any confusion you may have about belonging to one.

WHAT REALLY IS A CHURCH?

As soon as you say the word "church" people usually think of a building with a steeple on top of it. This, in fact, is not a church at all. It's a church building.

When the Bible talks about a church, it's simply referring to a group of Christians meeting together. In fact, the word originally meant "gathering". The very first Christians used to gather together in someone's house. It wasn't until a couple of centuries later that they decided to make huge buildings to meet in.

It's important to make this clear. A church is a group of Christians who meet together to strengthen one another's faith in God. With this in mind, they listen to God (through hearing the Bible read and taught), they respond to God (in prayer and praise) and they encourage each other (through conversations) to grow as Christians.

WHY GO TO CHURCH?

This chapter started with the question, "Must I go to church?" The answer is yes and no. On the one hand, you do not have to go to church to become a Christian, but on the other, you might not survive very long as a Christian unless you have the support church can give.

When I say that you don't have to go to church to be a Christian, I simply mean that God doesn't get excited every time you go to church and think to himself, "Wow, they're good, I'd better let them be my children". There is nothing we can do to earn the name Christian. It is a gift from God. He forgives us, makes us completely new, gives us a place in his kingdom and becomes our friend, all because of what Christ did on the cross. So then, going to church does not make you a Christian any more than sleeping in a garage makes you a car.

So why church? Here are a few reasons why belonging to a church is a great idea.

1. YOU WILL LEARN

One of the best reasons for belonging to a church is that you will learn a great deal of important stuff. When I first became a Christian, I was amazed by the whole thing and wanted to know everything I possibly could about Jesus. What I learnt from the minister and other Christians at my church laid a solid foundation for my life. It kept me going during the difficult times and drew me heaps closer to God. Jesus once said:

> **Therefore everyone who hears these words of mine and puts them into practice is like a wise man who built his house on the rock. The rain came down, the streams rose, and the winds blew and beat against that house; yet it did not fall, because it had its foundation on the rock. But everyone who hears these words of mine and does not put them into practice is like a foolish man who built his house on sand. The rain came down, the streams rose, and the winds blew and beat against that house, and it fell with a great crash.**   **Matthew 7:24-27**

I guarantee, there is no better way to learn about Jesus' words and how to put them into practice than belonging to a good church.

2. YOU WILL MEET PEOPLE

Of course, learning isn't the only good reason for belonging to a church. Another advantage is the people you'll meet. Some of my best friends have been people I've met at church. We are able to help out and challenge each other as Christians.

At rough times in my Christian life, the support and encouragement of my Christian friends has helped me hang in there. Having people around who listened to my doubts and struggles (and there were heaps) was a fantastic thing.

I don't want to give you the idea that belonging to a church or having Christian friends is all about having 'deep and meaningfuls' all the time. It is actually much more than that. Church is the best place to talk openly with a wide range of people about your goals and hopes, about how great God is, or about things you want others to pray for.

3. YOU CAN HELP OTHERS

Let us consider how we may spur one another on toward love and good deeds. Let us not give up meeting together...but let us encourage one another-and all the more as you see the Day approaching.

Hebrews 10:24-25

Church is not simply a place where you 'get'. It's a place where you 'give'. I'm not just referring to your money. I'm talking about giving yourself–your time, your listening ear, your abilities–everything, for the sake of your brothers and sisters in God's family. Jesus said:

A new commandment I give you: love one another. As I have loved you, so you must love one another. **John 13:34**

When we become Christians, we join a family–God's family–with brothers and sisters of all ages and types. Now it's pretty hard to love the other members of your family if you never actually get around to spending any time with them. We go to church in order to love other Christians–to encourage them in their Christian lives in whatever way we can.

Some people feel as though they are useless and could never contribute anything to the family. Let me make clear, no matter who you are or what you can do, if you are willing to be used, God can and will use you. There are heaps of things to be done to contribute to your church and to encourage other people. We usually concentrate on the 'up front' things like singing or leading, but looking out for each other and talking to people is just as important. Once you become more comfortable in your church, you might take the initiative to sit next to someone who's new or a bit lonely and talk to them.

If you do have some kind of talent or ability (e.g., singing or leading or drama), then quietly let your minister or youth leader know. Don't go around telling everyone how wonderful you are, but don't be shy about it either. If you have a good attitude (not too proud of yourself) and talents that you are willing to use, they can be extremely beneficial to the rest of the church.

The Bible says that God's Spirit has given Christians different gifts for the common good. These can be seen as supernatural gifts or abilities, but from God's point of view they are quite natural.

> **Now to each one the manifestation of the Spirit is given for the common good.**   **1 Corinthians 12:7**

It is clear from this verse that each Christian has at least one of these gifts. However, it is important to understand that these gifts do not indicate how 'spiritual' you are. For example, the Christian who has a great gift for teaching is no better than the Christian who has the simple gift of encouraging people. A gift only lets you know how great the Giver is, not the receiver. The following passage lists some of the gifts found in the Bible.

> **Now to each one the manifestation of the Spirit is given for the common good. To one there is given through the Spirit the message of wisdom, to another the message of knowledge by means of the same Spirit, to another faith by the same Spirit, to another gifts of healing by that one Spirit, to another miraculous powers, to another prophecy, to another distinguishing between spirits, to another speaking in different kinds of tongues, and to still another the interpretation of tongues. All these are the work of one and the same Spirit, and he gives them to each one, just as he determines.**   **1 Corinthians 12:7-11**

If you are at all confused about this stuff, ask your minister or some older Christian friends to help you find the gift God has given you for the benefit of others.

Attending my church is such a buzz because I know that I'll learn something new, catch up with my Christian friends, and that God may even use me to help out in some way.

There are probably other reasons why going to church is a good thing but the three points mentioned are hopefully enough to show that church does not have to be a total bore. In fact it can be just the opposite.

CHOOSING A CHURCH

There are big ones, small ones, loud ones, quiet ones and exciting ones. Some churches are still and stuffy, and others are more like an aerobics session. At some the speaker is funny and interesting, at others he is serious or maybe speaks too long.

There are heaps of different types of churches around this country, so how do you find a good one?

A lot of the choice is up to you and your personal taste. Some people love a quiet church service, others love an active kind of service where everyone participates. These sort of differences don't matter very much. There are a few guidelines, though, that you should follow to ensure that the church you choose will help you grow as a Christian. These guidelines are much more important than the 'style' of the meeting or the dress sense of the minister.

Here are four questions you might want to ask yourself about a church you are considering.

1. DO THEY TEACH FROM THE BIBLE?

A good church teaches regularly from the Bible and considers it to be the true account of God's plan for us. Many people have gone astray into awful beliefs because their church did not teach from the Bible as the single authority on the Christian faith.

There are so many weird ideas floating around the world today that if a church does not stick to what the Bible says, it might become like a boat in a storm without an anchor. If a church does not hold this view of the Bible, or even has other books it thinks are just as important, keep away.

2. DO THEY HELP OTHERS KNOW HOW TO BECOME CHRISTIANS?

A good church is always keen and active in spreading the Christian message. After all, one of the main reasons God chooses to bless people is so that they can pass the blessing on to others.

3. IS THE CHURCH CENTRED ON JESUS?

The Bible says of Jesus:

> He is the image of the invisible God, the firstborn over all creation. For by
> him all things were created: things in heaven and on earth, visible and
> invisible, whether thrones or powers or rulers or authorities; all things
> were created by him and for him. He is before all things, and in him all
> things hold together. And he is the head of the body, the church.
>
> **Colossians 1:15-18**

These words make it pretty clear what place Jesus should occupy in our church (and personal life). He is the head of the church and should dominate our thoughts, teaching, singing, prayers–everything. If everything is held together by Jesus, as this Scripture says, a church would do well to concentrate on him.

4. DO THEY HAVE A GENUINE LOVE AND CONCERN FOR EACH OTHER?

Jesus said:

> By this all men will know that you are my disciples, if you love one
> another.   John 13:35

A 'Jesus church' is a loving one. Each church has different opportunities and different circumstances, but there should always be an attitude of love and concern. I don't mean a corny kind of love; I mean real love that shows itself in actions.

If you follow these guidelines I'm sure you'll soon find a church to belong to. Remember, though, don't be too picky or judgemental. You will never find a 'perfect' church because churches are made up of people like me, and you.

BE PART OF THE TEAM

A footy player who avoids going to training and never hangs out with his team will probably never feel part of that team. When the weekend game comes around, he'll find it hard to hang in there for the whole match and when the play gets rough, he'll probably crumble. When Christians try to survive on their own, without belonging to a church, they are likely to encounter similar problems with their faith.

God wants all of us to belong to a church, not because we 'have' to, but because he knows we need it. He knows that in a church situation we can develop as Christians, and together have a significant effect on this needy world.

> **Check These Out**
> ► 1 Cor 12-14   ► Acts 2:42-47

"OUR KID'S GONE WEIRD"
Living with parents who aren't Christians

THIS CHAPTER IS for those, who still live at home and whose parent(s) don't quite 'love' the idea of their children becoming Christians, or even worse, remaining one.

I consider myself to be an expert in the area of relating to parents who aren't Christians. I say this because I am probably the best example you are ever likely to meet of what *not* to be. I have made so many mistakes in this area that I am positive you will benefit from my stupidity.

AVOIDING THE 'WEIRD' FACTOR

One of the first concerns of a parent whose son or daughter has 'gotten religious' is the fear that their baby has been brainwashed into some weird new cult. This is quite understandable, really. In Australia today there are many strange religious groups who on the surface appear 'nice' but are actually very deceptive and destructive. You only have to watch *60 Minutes* or *A Current Affair* (and parents do) to see what I mean.

Now, it might be a well-kept secret amongst young Australians, but broadly speaking, parents genuinely love their kids. As a result, they do not want anything 'weird' to take over their son or daughter. This is why it is very important to make clear to your parents that you have not joined the 'Children of Universal God-Hood' or some other bizarre cult,

but have actually become a normal, Bible-believing Christian and are going to a normal, Bible-believing church. If not convinced by your own words, ask them if they would like to meet the church minister or youth worker or some other person from the church. An informal afternoon tea or dinner with a Christian their age will go a long way to easing your parents' minds about your faith. If that sounds too difficult, simply invite some of the people your own age over to your place when you know your parents are likely to be home. That way, at least your folks can see that at church you are mixing with a bunch of normal, healthy and sensible people.

This is very, very important. The more your parents know about your church and faith, the less suspicious they will be. You never know, God could even use such a meeting to bring your parents to know him.

COPPING AND COPING WITH CRITICISM

Criticism from parents is often the most hurtful kind you will experience. This is true whether the criticism is about our sporting attempts or physical appearance. From time to time, I meet people who struggle with very real insecurities because their parents have too frequently compared them to the much better looking and/or smarter sister or brother. It's enough to leave a deep impression for many years.

Now, there is a good reason why comments from our parents will affect us more deeply than most. You see, it is generally true that for most of our younger years, parents were our constant security and trustworthy guide. We looked to them for just about everything–for protection when we were in danger, for answers when we were confused, and for love when we were hurt. This is the way God intended things to be. We are meant to be profoundly dependent on our parents, because, for the most part, their love for us makes them greatly dependable. Now, this dependence on parents is the reason for their influence on us. It's an influence that you will probably never completely shake (unless, of course, there has been some horrible fracture in the relationship), and nor should you.

The problem, however, is that this influence can sometimes be used in ways that God didn't intend. This brings me to my point: when parents criticise us about our faith in God, the effect is usually very painful.

It's important to understand this because comments from Mum or Dad like, "Oh, Christianity is a load of rubbish..." or "It's just a phase–you'll snap out of it", can send the average Christian spinning into a time of great doubt. There is no easy way to handle such comments, and they may never improve. If they come, they will hurt. I can't really offer a solution. I just hope that by raising the issue and explaining why their comments can be so hurtful, you will at least be prepared for the pain. The last thing you should do, though, is react aggressively by saying something like, "Yeah, well you're just blind and you're gonna fry in hell if you don't accept God". Regardless of whether it's true or not, this kind of reply will do more to keep them away from Jesus than it will to bring them to him.

Remember, God is always aware of your needs and he will never leave you to handle such situations alone. Psalm 27:10 reads:

> **Though my father and mother forsake me, the Lord will receive me.**

Jesus himself said:

> **Blessed are you when people insult you, persecute you and falsely say all kinds of evil against you because of me. Rejoice and be glad, because great is your reward in heaven, for in the same way they persecuted the prophets who were before you.**   **Matthew 5:11-12**

THE ART OF DISOBEDIENCE

Before becoming a Christian, much of my time was spent disobeying my teachers, scout leader, soccer coach and, of course, my mother. In fact, the only person I decided not to disobey was my martial arts instructor. There were some very sane reasons behind that decision.

Although my Mum was, and still is, a very caring parent, I was a real jerk and tried to turn disobedience into an art form. When I became a Christian however, I knew that things had to change. I was confronted with a very awkward Bible passage which read:

> **Children, obey your parents in everything, for this pleases the Lord.**   **Colossians 3:20**

I tried to convince myself that you only had to obey your parents if they were Christians, but no matter how I looked at it, the truth was clear–I had to learn to obey Mum and respect her wishes above my own. I was much better at disobedience than obedience but my attitude certainly did undergo a major change. I learnt that obeying parents pleases God (it also pleases them) and that's a good enough reason to do anything.

On a practical level, this means not deceiving them. It also means doing the jobs around the house. From time to time, it may even mean changing your social schedule to fit into their wishes! Yes, even the social schedule!

Now a question arises at this point: "What if my parents want me to do things that keep me from God?" This is a very difficult question to answer in a book this small but I will relate some examples which may help to make the issue clearer.

Example number one: Suppose you are in your room praying one evening and your dad calls from the kitchen, "I want you to help me with the dishes...now!" What should you do? Should you do the 'spiritual' thing and keep praying? Or should you do the 'earthly' thing and wash the stupid dishes? The answer is simple: do the truly spiritual thing and get into the kitchen, quick smart! In cases like this, God would much rather we pleased our parents than annoy them. Besides, you can always pray while you do the dishes, or some time later. This is a very important point.

Example number two: What if your parents forbid you to belong to a church?

This has never been my personal experience, but I have spoken to a number of people for whom this has been a real problem. There is no simple answer to this question, since each situation will have different circumstances. Generally, though, I think that if your parents absolutely command you not to go to church, you must respect their wishes. This may not be as tragic as it sounds. God knows your situation and he is able to support and teach you in other ways. For instance, a Christian group at school or uni can often be a huge source of strength if church is not an option. God may even just bring along some great Christian friends.

Either way, he will not leave you alone.

Thankfully, most of us will never have to deal with situations this tough, but the challenge still remains to obey our parents in the smaller things from day to day.

To avoid any confusion I must make two further points. Firstly, there will come a time when obeying parents will no longer be strictly applicable. I can't imagine a thirty year-old married son, for instance, continuing to obey his parents' every wish.

Secondly, there are some circumstances where children must disobey their parents. For example, God does not expect a son or daughter to consent to sexual, physical or psychological abuse from a parent (or anyone). If this is your situation, tell someone mature and respectable–a teacher, a youth leader, a minister. Don't let it continue. You must do something about it for your sake and your parents'. Of course, telling someone will be very difficult but problems are never solved by ignoring them and bottling them up.

TELLING THEM ABOUT JESUS

In the last few years, I've had the privilege of explaining my faith to students, teachers, Hare Krishnas, drug addicts, prisoners and others, but none have been as hard to talk with about Jesus as my own Mum.

I'm sure this has been the experience of millions of young Christians around the world ever since Jesus walked the earth. It's not that parents are particularly stubborn people, it's just that they're...'parents'.

Well, how do you talk to parents about Jesus? And do they ever respond and become Christians?

A couple of my friends' parents have listened to the Gospel message and have become Christians. The mum of a friend of mine is a good example. Partly through the example of her son and partly through being invited to church a few times, she has come to trust and follow Jesus. Sadly, though, this doesn't happen every day. Because of their authority over us, not only do we find it hard telling parents, but they find it hard listening.

Taking 'advice' (bad word, but that's how they see it) from a child on any topic is hard enough for a parent. Being told they need to ask God for mercy is just too much. It can be particularly hard if they've had some Christian contact in their childhood and now think they are an expert.

For this reason, I suggest four things.

1. BE CAREFUL NOT TO NAG OR PREACH TO YOUR PARENTS

Instead, look for opportunities in conversations and just say what you can about Jesus, without Bible-bashing. If they close up the topic, just let it go.

When I toured with the band, I would occasionally write to my Mum and mention briefly what I'd been doing. I'd mention what I sang and spoke about at the last school or prison I visited. This was not preaching but it kept Mum mildly aware of my faith. I'm not saying that you need to be sneaky about it either. Just openly share what you can and respect your parents' tolerance level, which is often not very high.

2. PRAY FOR YOUR PARENTS

This is silent but effective. Ultimately, it is God who does the work of bringing people into relationship with himself. He hears your prayers, so ask him continually to bring your parents to faith in Jesus.

3. TRY INVITING YOUR PARENTS TO CHURCH OCCASIONALLY

This may sound impossible but just choose a suitable meeting. For example, most churches occasionally put on special visitors' services. These are usually geared for 'unchurched' people. Also, if you ever do a singing spot at church or something similar, invite your parents to come and watch. As I said before, don't nag them. If they say no, just leave it and ask them another time. You never know, your church could be just the right place for your parents to hear the great news about Jesus.

4. STRIVE TO LOVE AND OBEY YOUR PARENTS

If you sincerely want your parents to think highly of Jesus, they first need to think highly of the influence Christianity is having in your life. Believe me, you are far more likely to see your parents become Christians with a tea towel in your hand than a Bible. One of my deepest regrets is not having learnt this earlier in my Christian life. A bad example as a Christian does lots to harden a parent's attitude toward Jesus, but a good example can do lots to soften a parent's view of him.

Being a Christian in a non-Christian environment is not always easy. As God's child though, it is your special privilege and duty to be his representative in your family. Remember, Jesus himself once lived in a family too. What kind of son do you think he would have been?

Check These Out

▶ Prov 10:1

▶ Eph 6:2-3

MISSIONARY DATING
Romance with a non-Christian

I AM OFTEN ASKED THE question, "Is it wrong to 'go out' with someone who is not a Christian?" Along with this I hear comments like, "There are no boys at my church", or "All the girls are gross". I've never actually heard a sermon on 'Romance and the Christian', nor read anything that provides much guidance for people in these situations. So I warn you there is not a vast amount of research invested into this chapter. It is just a collection of advice gathered from experience and from many of my smart friends.

The issue is not an easy one. There is no real black or white answer. The Bible does warn against marrying someone who doesn't follow Christ, but it doesn't even touch on the subject of 'going out'. (This is probably because 'going out' is a more recent thing.) For this reason, I cannot be dogmatic but only offer an opinion that hopefully makes (common) sense.

MISSIONARY DATING?

When I speak to Christians who are going out with someone who does not share the same belief, they often tell me how much good it will do their partner: "I'll help him/her become a Christian…she/he even came to church with me last week".

Admittedly, this sounds great, and the sincerity of the point is clear. However, I must say that I have never seen this kind of 'action plan' work out. There have been rare occasions where the girlfriend or boyfriend shows a definite interest in becoming a Christian, but it usually dies when the relationship dies.

My own experience may help make things clearer. In the years after becoming a Christian I had relationships with two or three lovely girls who did not share my beliefs. Each time, I convinced myself and others (and even tried convincing God) that I could help these 'poor lost souls' find Jesus. To be honest, the plan backfired.

For about the first month, I was confident that my 'missionary tactics' would work. However, I soon found myself so obsessed with the 'love of my life' that I almost forgot about Jesus. No-one told me that this might happen, so I learnt the hard way.

Now don't get me wrong. I'm not blaming the girls. They were fantastic people. It's just that when one person in the relationship doesn't share the belief of the other, it makes things very difficult. Either the belief will fizzle to make room for the love, or the love will fizzle to make room for the belief. I've experienced both and they are equally painful. Some of my closest friends have also tried this 'missionary dating' and have ended up succeeding in the 'dating' and forgetting the 'mission'. Romance with a non-Christian may not be wrong, but trying to bring them to Christ is certainly a 'mission improbable'.

Do not be yoked together with unbelievers...What does a believer have in common with an unbeliever?   **2 Corinthians 6:14-15**

This verse is not saying that we should avoid contact with non-Christians. It's not even a direct reference to romantic relationships. However, it does reveal an important fact–believers and unbelievers don't have a whole lot in common on a spiritual level. They are like two people walking on different roads. It makes it very difficult to relate. Sure, they may both listen to silverchair or U2, but when it comes to the deeper issues of faith in God and commitment to him, they might as well be in different solar systems.

A BETTER PLAN

Whether or not it's wrong to get romantically involved with a guy/girl who's not a Christian, I'll leave for others to fight out. My settled opinion now is far more simple and practical.

If you are a Christian and single and you really want a partner, why settle for second best? By 'second best' I do not mean that Christians are great people and everyone else is bad. I simply mean that a relationship between two Christians who put God first will naturally be more fulfilling than a relationship of differing beliefs and priorities.

Romance is not our invention–it's God's. In fact, there's a whole book in the Bible devoted to the topic of passionate, sexual, romantic love. If two people love their Creator and treat one another the way he designed, it makes sense that their relationship will experience a deep level of enjoyment. It's not simply that they both share a common 'hobby'. They share a common Lord. More than a hobby (though some Christians treat it like one), Christianity is a new life, heading towards eternal life. When two people 'in love' know this life for themselves, there is a bond and dimension to the relationship that is incomparable. It's a relationship by the Manufacturer's instructions.

Realizing this fact, a number of my Christian friends have refused to settle for second best, and have waited until the right girl (or guy) came into their lives–someone with whom they can pray, talk about their faith and who will challenge them in that faith. This may sound corny but to those who have experienced this kind of relationship, it is by far the better plan.

Some time ago, one of my closest friends fell for a guy who was not a Christian. He was a top bloke and was even willing to listen to her explanation of her faith in Jesus but he didn't accept Jesus for himself. For a number of weeks she struggled with her own feelings of love, and guilt for having that love. She is a very mature Christian but found herself torn two ways. "Do I go out with this guy (who certainly returned her feelings) or do I stop seeing him as I feel I should." Finally, after some very hard and painful thinking, she rang him to say she would no longer see him in a romantic situation. She still had deep feelings for this guy for a long while afterwards (I firmly believe there is no wrong in that) but she didn't allow her feelings to govern her life. Her Lord governed her life. It was hard but there is a peace in doing what you feel is right that brings comfort to any hurt. As it turns out, she later found another top bloke who was just as devoted to Jesus as she was. I went to their wedding a few days ago.

Then, of course, there's the 'problem' of not being able to find a partner. What if there are no Christian guys or girls on the scene, or the ones that are around are not interested in you? It's great to have a partner but I think we've been sucked into believing that if you don't have one, you're some kind of alien. That is not the case at all. If you find yourself in this situation, don't get too down about it and whatever you do, don't go looking for just anyone to fill the space. I think some Christians feel frustrated by not having a girlfriend or boyfriend and end up going out with someone who doesn't believe simply because they can't be bothered waiting. Hang in there; don't get too intense. Instead, trust God who knows all your needs and wants. Tell him how you feel, but whatever you do, don't take something you think is 'good' and miss out on the 'best'.

In the end, no-one can make your mind up for you. Either you will follow this advice and discover for yourself the value of Christian relationships or you will do it the hard way and learn as I learnt. Either way, God loves you and desires only good for you. In his time he'll get you to where he wants you.

TOO MUCH TOO YOUNG
About sex and stuff

"**C**AN WE PLEASE TALK?", she said with a worried tone in her voice as we sat on the steps outside a church in the Riverina district of NSW.

We talked for about half an hour, but all I remember is the flow of tears and the trembling voice, "I think I might be pregnant".

This pretty girl would have been fifteen at the oldest. Some weeks before, she and her boyfriend (both of whom were Christians) had made a decision. Probably not a calculated decision, but nevertheless, a decision.

At the time, they probably thought it was exciting–later there was regret. At the time, it probably seemed 'worth it'–later it was not.

I don't claim to be an expert on 'relationships and sex', and I do not intend to bore you with statistics like, "How many teenagers have had sexual intercourse before they leave high school?". Sorry! If you want that kind of information, go out and buy any issue of *Cleo* magazine.

Sex is something that Christians often struggle with. When I say 'struggle', I mean they often find it difficult knowing what is wrong, what is right, and 'how far you can go' before God is displeased. Like the last chapter, this is not a black and white issue, but hopefully these few pages will be of some help to those who sincerely want to honour God in their relationships.

THE BIG 'WHY NOT?'

People often ask, "Why doesn't God approve of sex?" In actual fact, God does approve of sex. He invented it. It's not like Adam and Eve discovered sex and said to themselves, "Wow, let's not tell God. He may get really annoyed". In his amazing creativity and love, God thought up a pretty intricate and pleasurable way for a man and a women to reproduce and enjoy one another.

The truth of the matter is that God has a far higher view of sex than you or me. The media has cheapened sexuality so much that it's hard to make a stand for the right enjoyment of sex without being laughed at as old fashioned and square.

An illustration may make this point clearer. I once owned a Datsun 1200. It wasn't worth much so I had no problem lending it out to anyone who wanted it. If they crashed it, it was no big deal. Suppose though, I owned a Porsche. I can assure you I wouldn't be lending it out. In fact, I'd be careful how I drove it myself. Such an expensive machine deserves that I would treat it with the utmost respect and care.

What I'm getting at is that in our modern world you will often hear a very 'Datsun' view of sex: "Lend it out. It's not that special". In God's eyes however, sex is far more like a Porsche. He sees it as valuable–so valuable that it must be kept for the right person. Far from being against sex, God is very much for it. This is why he has given us guidelines in the Bible for its enjoyment. People mock these guidelines, but only because they've been fooled into thinking that the 'Porsche' is a 'Datsun'.

> **So the LORD God caused the man to fall into a deep sleep; and while he was sleeping, he took one of the man's ribs and closed up the place with flesh. Then the LORD God made a woman from the rib he had taken out of the man, and he brought her to the man. The man said, "This is now bone of my bones and flesh of my flesh; she shall be called 'woman', for she was taken out of man." For this reason a man will leave his father and mother and be united to his wife, and they will become one flesh.**
>
> **Genesis 2:21-24**

This is the first description in the Bible of human sexuality. The statement forms the basis for our whole understanding of the topic. The phrase "one flesh" refers primarily to the sexual intimacy the husband and wife will enjoy. Notice, it says that once the two have become united (in marriage), then they become one flesh–not before. This is God's command. To break the command is to cheapen sexuality and displease God.

Apart from God's displeasure, there are other dangers in avoiding the Maker's instructions: sexually transmitted diseases, illegitimate babies, abortions, forced marriages or forced separations, family breakdowns and emotional scarring–these are just some of the possible results of sexual intercourse outside the commitment of the marriage relationship. Sure, today some of these problems can be avoided by using modern contraceptions but the risks are still real.

I once spoke with a girl in her early twenties who couldn't shake the hurt and guilt she felt from the abortion she had undergone a couple of years before. Her life was filled with shame and regret. There are no easy answers for situations like hers and all I could do was listen and assure her of God's love and willingness to forgive.

"But we love each other", I often hear. Of course you do. And if you love each other, you should care about the other person–you should care that they are honoured and respected, and not simply 'used' to satisfy your desires. If you love them, you should want what's best for them–and God says that what is best is leaving sex for marriage. Who is right: you or God?

Sexual intercourse is one of our Creator's finest inventions but it only finds his favour when enjoyed in the life-long commitment of a marriage relationship. Outside of this, we are violating the instructions of Almighty God. Trust God. Do what he says. It is always the best path leading to the best results.

PUSHING THE LIMITS

For many Christians, the question is not, "Why does God disapprove of sex (intercourse) outside marriage?" but rather, "How far can we push the limits?"

Some Christians ban all physical affection in their relationship, while others allow anything short of sexual intercourse. So who's right? The first opinion is safe, but in some people's minds, very boring. The second is probably fun, but also very dangerous and...well, wrong.

The following points are intended as helpful and practical hints in understanding the 'limits'. I want to be as blunt as I would be if I were speaking with you face to face because avoiding this issue will only cause more confusion.

AFFECTION VS. AROUSING

Much of the confusion among couples working out 'how far to go' is due to confusion between affection and arousing. How do you know when you've crossed the line from affectionate physical contact to sexual arousal? This question cannot be answered simply, as we all have different 'hot levels'. A passionate kiss to some people is a total bore, whereas others are driven wild by it. Only you know what your body is feeling at a given time and so only you can be the judge.

Affection is usually gentle and passive but arousal is more driving and active. Affection is emotionally based but arousal is more physically based. Because of these broad differences, we each should be able to gauge when we've 'crossed the line'. At that point, only honesty and haste will keep us from the 'no-go' zone.

What I am saying, basically, is this: expressing physical affection outside marriage is fine; sexually arousing one another is not. Our sexual desires are a normal part of our God-given personalities–they are good things, not evil. But they are very powerful (more so in some people than in others) and when we unleash them they are very hard to control. We should wait until we're married to let them loose and enjoy their power.

THE MOTIVE

One of the keys in recognizing the 'no-go' zone is to watch your motives. Behind affection is the idea of self-giving. Gestures such as kissing, cuddling, stroking hair, etc. are usually intended for the innocent enjoyment of the other person. It's a way of communicating love to your partner.

Sometimes, however, the motivation switches from self-giving to self-taking. When this occurs you can be sure that you're stepping over the line. It's an attempt to satisfy yourself sexually without much thought for the partner.

Included in the self-taking category is the attempt to turn your partner on. Although it appears to be 'giving', trying to excite your girlfriend/boyfriend is usually only an effort to influence them to let you go further, so in the end it is really quite selfish. The more they are 'turned on', the more likely they are to let you 'turn on' and so begins the cycle that often leads couples down the path of disobedience.

Prime tactics in this selfish game include rubbing yourself against your partner or simply rubbing them in sensitive areas. Beneath or above the clothes, very few people can remain 'turned off' when this kind of petting occurs. Affection is great, but when you find yourself less interested in giving and more interested in taking, it's probably time to cool off.

LOOK OUT FOR EACH OTHER

Biological research suggests that guys are generally (but certainly not always) more easily turned on than girls. It's important that girls realise this and act accordingly. Just because you may not be terribly excited doesn't mean your boyfriend isn't.

This, however, does not excuse the blokes. Just because we're generally weaker doesn't mean that we're any less responsible during close encounters.

Look out for each other. Watch the signs. It's not hard to tell what's going on when the talking stops and the breathing starts. If one of you is getting excited, the less occupied one should aim at cooling the situation down. A few casual words about the picture on the wall can sometimes dull a fiery moment. If not, try dropping a few lines about last Sunday's sermon in church.

The Bible says:

> **Flee the evil desires of youth, and pursue righteousness, faith, love and peace, along with those who call on the Lord out of a pure heart.**
>
> **2 Timothy 2:22**

Waiting until you get to the 'alarm-bells' stage that I've just described is actually quite irresponsible and often irreversible. We are told in this passage to run away from such situations. Rather than waiting, look out for each other by doing some pretty honest talking about your individual limits. Be open about what turns you on, and decide together not to do it. Make sure this is done at a very cool moment. If both of you know what the other has set as a limit, you will be far less eager to push those limits when the temptation arises. Actually, the common question, "How far can we go?" is completely the wrong question. It arises from a disobedient attitude that wants to go as far as it can without actually annoying God. The verse just quoted, however, insists that we run away from lust, not edge our way toward it.

Another thing that my wife and I found helpful during our three years of courting was a bracelet that I bought her to remind us of obedience to God. I gave it to her saying that it was a gift to represent holiness. Whenever we found ourselves in a tricky situation, there was this bracelet, rattling around her wrist reminding us both of our commitment to honour each other and not push the limits. It was not magic, but it certainly proved valuable to us.

It may sound obvious, but another really useful thing to do is to avoid tempting situations. Let's face it—we're all sinful, and given half the chance, we're just as likely to get carried away and do the wrong thing. Many young couples have found that simply by being a bit clever about where they spend their time together, they can avoid a lot of problems. If you don't give yourselves the time, the place and the opportunity, you're much less likely to be tempted. It's a bit hypocritical to pray "Do not lead me into temptation" and then go for a walk in the sand-dunes with your girlfriend on a dark moonless night with a beach-blanket. Who are you kidding?

There is probably much more that could be said on this subject but I hope this will be of some help to sincere couples.

God is not against sex. After all, he made it. He also designed the marriage relationship and only in that should we be sexually active. Until then, we should view our girlfriend/boyfriend as someone else's future wife or husband and treat them with unselfish love and respect. God is interested in your love life, and as long as you include and respect him in it, he will honour you with the kind of relationship that he intended.

Check These Out

▶ Matt 15:19-20   ▶ 1 Cor 6:18-20   ▶ 1 Cor 6:9-11

▶ Gal 5:19   ▶ 1 Thess 4:1-8

WHEN YOU FEEL LIKE A DOG
Can you trust how you feel?

EVERY NOW AND THEN I wake up in the morning feeling terrible. I'm tired, grumpy and feel very 'unspiritual'. It seems like God is having a bad day, and has decided to take it out on me.

It's not long until I remember, though, that God does not change–at all, ever! The mistake is mine–I trusted my feelings too much.

I often receive letters from Christians who struggle with similar problems. Some feel guilty for no apparent reason. Others feel that God has changed his mind about loving them. Then there are those who are confused as to why they don't feel as excited about God as they used to.

The common element in all these situations is the little word 'feel'. Should you trust how you feel? Is it a good guide to how you're going as a Christian?

These are tricky questions but if you can learn their answers and also live them out, you will be ten steps ahead in your Christian faith.

THE DANGER OF FEELINGS

There is a great danger in trusting your feelings to determine your 'spiritual level'. The danger is that feelings go up and down like a yo-yo.

If I have a bad day and come home feeling like God is keeping his distance from me, does that prove that God really is distant? Of course not! Jesus himself said, in Matthew 28:20, "...and I will be with you always..."

I met a person the other day who said, "God doesn't care about me". I asked, "How do you know?"

The reply was, "Cos I can't feel it".

Do her feelings indicate God's lack of care for her, even though his word makes it clear that he cares for everyone? Does her 'feeling' cancel out God's promise? Of course not! Feelings change. God does not.

If I were lost in the bush with a compass, I could either rely on my 'sense of direction' or on the needle pointing north. No matter how strongly I 'felt' about which direction to take, I'd be stupid to trust my feelings over the compass. Why? Because facts are far more reliable than feelings.

As you follow Christ, you will undoubtedly have good days and bad days or even good months and bad months. If you can learn to rely on the facts in the Bible, regardless of how you feel, you will save yourself from many unnecessary hassles.

Girls need to take special notice of this—not because they're moodier than blokes, but simply because their bodies affect them differently. God understands this and won't leave you to cope alone. He can be trusted.

Next time you "feel" that God is distant, or unloving, or whatever, turn to God's compass, the Bible. Believe it. Act upon it, because no matter what happens, God does not change. North is always north.

Jesus Christ is the same yesterday and today and forever.   Hebrews 13:8

The appendix at the back of the book may help you to use God's compass. There you'll find lots of Bible verses for different occasions. Look them up, think about them, believe them—look north.

THE ROLE OF FEELINGS

If I gave you a thousand dollars, you would probably feel pretty happy. If I pointed a loaded gun at your head you would probably feel a bit scared. Certain facts bring about certain feelings. In some cases, it is almost impossible to believe something without feelings being stirred.

This is where feelings come into our lives as Christians. Although I've already warned about the dangers of trusting feelings over facts, the other side of the coin is this: if the facts about God and his plan for us remain as cold information in our heads, our Christian faith will lack energy. We must allow the facts to get into our emotions as well as our brains.

If you are a child of God, you are forgiven and are assured of a place in God's future Kingdom. Surely you should occasionally 'feel' good about this. I mean, I get excited about going on holidays, but no holiday compares to where I'll be going when I die.

If you find that your faith is a bit cold or stale, I suggest you spend some time reading over the facts in the Bible.

For example, if I ever feel unloved by God, I turn to a verse like Psalm 103:11:

> **For as high as the heavens are above the earth, so great is His love for those who fear Him.**

I'll sit down and think about it, thank God for it and ask him to help me grasp it. This often helps it sink into my head. The fact doesn't change but my understanding of it does.

So then, trust God's facts not your feelings, but don't be surprised if as you study the Bible you get excited in the process.

I BELIEVE, I THINK!
The dilemma of doubts

SEVERAL YEARS AGO I was walking through a Christian bookstore when a title caught my eye: DOUBT. I turned to make sure no-one was looking and nervously skimmed across the pages, hoping to find some magical cure to a problem I had battled with for ages.

Doubt is one of those funny subjects that not too many of us like to talk about. It's as if we think avoiding the issue will make it go away. Not so! Doubt is a harmful critter and needs to be tackled head-on.

"Can I still be a Christian if I doubt?"

"Is it sinful?"

"How do I stop?"

These are questions often asked by doubt-crippled Christians. Hopefully, I can answer them in the next few pages.

The Oxford Dictionary says that doubt is "a feeling of uncertainty". Doubt in the Christian life is a feeling of uncertainty about God, or something he has said in his word. As far as I can see, there are four major types of doubt. Proud doubt, brain doubt, slack doubt and worry doubt. The first step in overcoming doubt is to recognise which type it is.

PROUD DOUBT

Proud doubt is a refusal to accept some truth about God. It stems from an attitude that says, "I know better than God". I've not met too many Christians who suffer from this. It is usually people who think that believing in God will cramp their style. For instance, some people say, "I don't believe in God because he doesn't like us getting drunk". That's about as stupid as saying, "I don't believe in that cyclone because it's going to wreck my house".

Refusing to believe is a choice, and when we refuse to believe God, it is a wrong choice.

BRAIN DOUBT

The second type of doubt is very different from proud doubt. Instead of being a *refusal* to believe, 'brain doubt' is when you find it *difficult* to believe something about God and his book. This is often the result of a lack of investigation or understanding in a particular area.

A number of years ago, I began to question how reliable the Bible was. People told me 'it had changed' and was 'more like a fairy tale' than a true account of God's plan.

I began to do some study, reading about how the Bible came together and found that I had absolutely nothing to worry about. It would have been very easy to ignore my doubts and not do the study but this would have only led to more doubt and confusion later on.

Sometimes, 'brain doubt' can come from not really understanding who God is and what it means to be a Christian. I meet a lot of Christians who really doubt whether they are Christians at all. They might doubt that God really accepts them (because they've done something bad) or that the quality of their Christian life is good enough. I usually tell people to go back to

square one and look at what the Bible says about how you become a Christian–that it is by trusting in Christ; that God loves and accepts and forgives us because of the huge value of Christ's death, not because of the quality of our lives.

If you suffer from this type of doubt, put your brain into gear and do a bit of investigating. Ask a Christian friend, or a minister, for a good book on whatever subject you may doubt. Remember, God is not worried about being found out a phoney, because he's not one.

WORRY DOUBT

This is more complex than the last two types of doubt and is often much harder to deal with. Before I explain 'worry doubt', let me give you an everyday example of it in action.

Suppose you are head over heels in love with someone who doesn't appear to return your feelings. Then a mutual friend tells you that this person does, in fact, have a crush on you. Your initial reaction might be, "Oh, no way–they couldn't love me".

Now, does this doubt arise because you question your friend's truthfulness? Probably not. It is far more likely to be a defence mechanism to keep you from a possible letdown. So much hangs on the other person liking you back that your mind protects you with 'worry doubt'.

Likewise, some Christians (usually quite committed ones) suffer from a similar problem. So much depends on their faith being true that their minds play tricks on them and occasionally say "Is God really there?", "Am I just kidding myself?", "Am I a Christian?", "Maybe God doesn't love me", etc.

It is not 'proud doubt' or 'brain doubt' but a kind of defence mechanism that protects us from being let down. Our emotions can play a strong part in this. They can rise up and give us a hard time (see chapter 10).

Another example of 'worry doubt' may make it clearer.

Years ago, the band I play in was invited to perform overseas at a large music festival. Before we went on stage, my mind was filled with doubts like, "I can't do this" and "I hope we don't blow it". It wasn't that

I didn't think I could sing or perform, it was simply 'worry doubt' rearing its ugly head because so much hung on our first overseas performance.

The concert ended up going very well. I really had nothing to worry about in the first place. Likewise, if you struggle with worry doubt in your Christian life, don't despair. God is aware of your doubts and wants you to relax. He is holding on to you tighter than you are holding on to him.

SLACK DOUBT

There's one last kind of doubt I want to mention. 'Slack doubt' arises not from some intellectual problem or from worry or emotions. It drifts into our minds over time when we're being slack as Christians.

When we don't exercise our faith–when we put it on hold and just get on with our everyday lives–our trust in God grows weak. We drift away from God, bit by bit, so that we hardly notice, until one day we start doubting whether he's really there, or whether we were ever really Christians at all, and so on. This uncertainty is a direct result of our slackness, and the remedy for it is simple but brutal–we've got to get our act together and start trusting God again.

OVERCOMING DOUBTS

Having described these different types of doubt, let me offer some suggestions as to how to beat them.

Mark 9:17-27 tells the story of a bloke who came to Jesus one day begging him to heal his son. Jesus replied, "Everything is possible for him who believes". In despair the man cried, "I do believe; help me overcome my unbelief!"

The man three-quarters believed and one-quarter doubted. It would have been very easy for him to sit around all day doubting and worrying about his son but he never would have met Jesus. He didn't sit around though. Instead, he thought to himself, "Blow this, I'm going to Jesus, doubts and all". The story ends with Jesus healing the son.

This is not a bad example to follow. It teaches a great lesson about how to beat doubts. The lesson is this: always side with faith, not doubt.

If the father had concentrated on his doubts too much, he might have lost the opportunity to see Jesus' power and trustworthiness. Instead, he sided with faith regardless of his doubts and went home on top of the world.

If 'proud doubt' is your problem, side with faith–stop refusing God and trust him. If 'brain doubt' gets you down, side with faith–do some study. If 'worry doubt' is your struggle, again, side with faith–don't dwell on doubts but relax and trust our big God. And finally, if you're troubled by 'slack doubt', side with faith–trust God enough to put him first in your life.

Doubts aren't necessarily wrong (unless it is proud doubt). It is what you do with them that counts. As someone once said, "Doubts are like birds; you can't stop them flying overhead but you can stop them nesting in your hair".

Check These Out

▶ Luke 17:5-9

▶ Heb 11:1

▶ Prov 3:5

THE DEVIL AND CO.

About satan, demons, etc

HAVE YOU EVER NOTICED at a party or some other gathering, that as soon as someone talks about Satan or demons, everyone instantly tunes in?

There is a fascination in our society with the Devil, particularly amongst younger people. There are hundreds of bands, T-shirts, film clips, posters, occult shops, all in the business of 'selling the Devil'.

Touring with the band I've discovered that about seven out of ten schools and universities have something about Satan written on the back of toilet doors (I can only speak for guys toilets, of course).

Things like 'God Sux. Satan Rules', '666, the number of the beast', or 'Satan lives'.

Every now and then some bloke in the front row of our concerts would hold up his hand to make the sign of the Devil (fist closed, pointer and pinky outstretched). I think it was meant to scare me, so usually I'd move across stage, right in front of them and stare them out while singing extra loudly about Jesus. At this they always stopped and often died of embarrassment.

Unfortunately, there are an awful lot of misconceptions about the Devil and co. In this chapter, I want to do some damage to the Devil and look at who he really is, what he does and how we as Christians should deal with him.

THE DEVIL AND DEMONS

The Bible is not crystal clear as to how the Devil came about except that he seems to have been an angel that went bad. The word Satan means 'enemy' and Devil means 'accuser'. Both words describe pretty well who this 'being' is and what he is like. He is God's arch-enemy (though not a threat to him) and because of God's special concern for us, he is our enemy also.

The Bible makes it clear that only God is all-powerful, all-knowing and everywhere. This means that Satan cannot do everything he wants, know everything he wants, nor be everywhere he wants. He is a very powerful, but also very limited, spirit being. By 'spirit being', I simply mean he does not have a permanent body like you or me. It's important to realise, however, that although he has a 'spiritual existence', this enemy can still influence our physical world. More about this later.

The Bible also talks about lesser evil spirits called 'demons'. They seem to be sort of like Satan's offsiders or henchmen. The Devil could be seen as the General in a fierce army, and demons as the lower ranks who help in the war.

THE DEVIL'S WORK

One of the problems in writing such a brief book is trying to decide what to say and what to leave out. The work of Satan is so varied that it is only possible to give a quick overview of his schemes. The following points are a brief summary of the insight God's word gives us into the work of the Devil.

BLINDING

Of all Satan's plans, none is more evil and destructive than what we read of in 2 Corinthians 4:4:

The god of this age (the devil) has blinded the minds of unbelievers, so that they cannot see the light of the gospel...

Here we are told that Satan prevents people from understanding the gospel message. He blinds them in a spiritual sense. I've seen this a lot. Sometimes I've been over and over the Christian message with someone who wants to understand but they've seemed unable to grasp it.

One of my closest friends found herself on the raw end of this Satanic trick for many months. She used to say, "Something is holding me back but I don't know what". Finally, one night something clicked and all that she had learnt about Christ suddenly made sense. She's now a very mature and devoted Christian. When talking to others about God's salvation, we need to be aware of the Devil's tactics and pray that God will help them to understand.

CONTROLLING

1 John 5:19 says:

We know that we are children of God, and that the whole world is under the control of the evil one.

It may sound outrageous but in this verse we are told that everyone (except God's children) is under the Devil's control. Now before we run out and tell everyone that the Devil controls them, we need to understand that this does not mean that every bad thing a person does is the Devil's doing. We are not told exactly how Satan controls people, but you can be sure it explains an awful lot of the evil in the world today.

POSSESSING?

Demon possession may be a good plot for a movie but sadly it is quite often misunderstood. Demons can and do hold influence over some people, but they don't actually own people, as the word 'possession' seems to imply. We see many examples of demonised people in the first five books of the New Testament. Luke 9:37-42 is a typical example. In this case, demons had driven a man to the point of madness, controlling his thoughts and altering his hold on reality. It's important to note that demons can only exert this type of influence in people's lives when the person has given their consent, or left an opening in their lives. This is why seances and other such things are very dangerous. Stay away from them.

It is also important for Christians to realize that because God's Spirit lives in them, they need not worry about being 'possessed'. The Bible says:

> **For he has rescued us from the dominion of darkness and brought us into the kingdom of the Son he loves, in whom we have redemption, the forgiveness of sins.** Colossians 1:13-14

In other words, as a Christian you have been transferred out of the Devil's territory into God's territory. There is no possibility of Satan *controlling* one of God's children.

TEMPTING

Satan can still affect our lives as Christians. One of his favourite pastimes is tempting God's people to do wrong. I'm not saying that every time we disobey God it's the Devil's doing. We do still have the ability to choose right from wrong. It's just that from time to time, he will try to influence our circumstances to lead us towards wrong decisions. I say 'circumstances' not 'thoughts' because there is nothing in the Bible to suggest that the Devil can get inside your head and change your thinking. He can't work on you from the inside, only from the outside, bringing people and situations across your path that offer you the possibility of disobeying God.

INFLUENCING

In both Revelation 2:10 and 1 Thessalonians 2:18, we discover that Satan can influence physical circumstances in an attempt to hinder God's children. The first verse says:

> **Do not be afraid of what you are about to suffer. I tell you, the devil will put some of you in prison to test you, and you will suffer persecution for ten days.**

It appears that Satan was responsible for placing some of God's servants in prison. He probably did this by encouraging political officials to make immoral and unjust decisions about Christians.

In the second verse, we find that Satan actually prevented the Apostle Paul from visiting the Christians who lived in the region of Thessalonica:

> **For we wanted to come to you—certainly I, Paul, did, again and again—but Satan stopped us.**

We are not told how this was achieved but only that it was the Devil's doing.

It is important to realise that although Satan tries to hassle us in this way, God can turn it around for his own purposes. For example, even though Paul was prevented from visiting the Thessalonian church, it meant that he wrote them a letter instead. This letter then became a precious book of the Bible, full of great teaching for all God's children down through the centuries. The Devil lost badly.

DECEIVING

The very first act of the Devil recorded in the Bible involves him deceiving Eve about whether or not she should eat the fruit of the forbidden tree. Jesus said that the Devil is the "Father of all lies" (Jn 8:44). In other words, the central activity of the Devil is deceiving people. For Christians, this often takes the form of deceptive teaching about the Christian faith. The Apostle Paul in 2 Corinthians 11:3-4 says:

> **But I am afraid that just as Eve was deceived by the serpent's (Satan's) cunning, your minds may somehow be led astray from your sincere and pure devotion to Christ. For if someone comes to you and preaches a Jesus other than the Jesus we preached, or if you receive a different spirit from the one you received, or a different gospel from the one you accepted, you put up with it easily enough.**

In my travels, it has been one of my saddest experiences to find Christians who have accepted teaching not found in the Bible, or even stuff absolutely forbidden by it. It is very important that we keep to correct teaching. If you learn something that doesn't check out with what is written in the Bible, don't accept it. Far from it, expose it as lies. This applies to what you're reading now also. I've been very careful to do my best to explain what the Bible says, but if you find something in it that isn't biblical, rip that page out.

I cannot stress this enough–deception is the most deadly of the Devil's tactics. If Satan can bring some false teaching across your path (through a Christian book, a sermon, a friend, or whatever) and you choose to believe it, he will have you in a trap. For example, years ago I read a book that basically said that if I didn't wake up before sunrise each day and spend a good hour (at least) praying to God, I would miss out on the deeper blessings God has for me. I believed it, and tried to put it into practice. The result was that I missed out on sleep I needed and prayer became a guilt-ridden burden, not a privilege. The book taught lies which I believed. Satan was happy. Fortunately, a good friend of mine pointed out what the Bible does teach about prayer and God's blessing. I believed it and escaped the Devil's trap.

THE DEVIL AND US

In some of the movies where Satan has a starring role, you will often see some minister trying to stop the evil powers by praying and holding up wooden crosses or splashing 'holy water' around the place. Although the 'goodies' generally end up winning, I am always amazed at how much effort and how long it takes to beat the Devil. Even then, the victory is only a slight one. This is all wrong!

Before explaining how to deal with Satan, let me offer a word of warning. Christians usually fall for one of two errors when it comes to Satan (and Satan is probably behind both of them!). We either become obsessed with the Devil and see him everywhere, or else we ignore him completely as if he didn't exist. Satan isn't the cause of every bad thing or every sin, but neither is he non-existent. He "prowls around like a roaring lion" as it says in 1 Peter 5:8 and we need to be ready to resist his attacks.

How do we deal with Satan? We've got to start by realizing that basically, Satan is a 'loser' in the real sense of the word. I'm not saying he is weak or no cause for concern, but when it comes to God and God's children, he has already lost the war.

Hebrews 2:14 (Good News) says:

Jesus himself became like them (you and me) and shared their human nature. He did this so that through his death he might destroy the Devil...

When Jesus died on the cross, he accepted upon himself the consequences for all our disobedience and rejection of God. This meant that we could turn to God, receive complete forgiveness and be made righteous in his sight. When we become Christians, God transfers us from the Devil's 'kindom of darkness' into his own marvellous 'kingdom of light' (see Col 1:13-14). In other words, Jesus' death and resurrection destroyed the Devil's power to hold on to those who belong to God's kingdom. There's no need for 'holy water' or wooden crosses. The first key to dealing with Satan is simply to trust the fact that Christ has already defeated him.

James 4:7 says:

Submit yourselves, then, to God. Resist the devil, and he will flee from you.

In this verse we find two practical steps for getting rid of our enemy. Firstly, submit to God. This means recognizing him as the awesome Creator and putting him first in our lives. There can be no rejecting the Devil without submitting to God.

The second practical step to defeating the devil is to resist him. This includes recognizing that he is defeated by Christ, but it also means not giving in to the temptations and deceptions he brings across our paths. As we take these steps, the Devil doesn't just leave–he runs.

If you are a Christian, you're on the winning side. Not because you did anything great, but because Christ in his love died on the cross, to transfer you from Satan's grip to God's embrace.

Satan is a very real and evil enemy who has great power and many demons to work for him, but Christians don't have to fear him. He will undoubtedly try to hassle us from time to time, but we are already on top of the situation and will one day have the pleasure of watching God destroy Satan and his kingdom in the judgement awaiting them in Hell.

Check These Out

▶ Eph 6:11-17   ▶ 1 Pet 5:8-9   ▶ Rev 20:1-10

PLUGGED INTO GOD
About the Holy Spirit

AFTER ALL THE TALK of Satan and evil spirits in the previous chapter, it is probably a good idea to turn and look at the Holy Spirit. Most people have heard of the Holy Spirit in a hymn or a prayer or even a movie, but have no idea beyond that.

If you've been a Christian for a while, you might be aware that there are different views on this subject. These differing views are sometimes the cause of confusion among young Christians and arguments among 'older' ones. For this reason I won't enter into any controversial areas. Instead, I will simply explain what the Bible has to say about who the Holy Spirit is and what he does.

WHO IS HE?

You'll notice that the heading says, "Who is he?" not "What is it?". The Holy Spirit is not like 'the force' out of the Star Wars trilogy. He is a person. In fact, more than a person, he is none other than God himself. God exists as three individuals: Father, Son and Holy Spirit. Although they are separate, they are all one and the same. Sounds weird I know, but God's Word is very clear on this point.

In the Bible, the Holy Spirit is given a number of names. These names give us insight into his character. For example, the "Spirit of Christ" (Rom 8:9) implies his exact likeness to the character of Jesus Christ. Some others include: the "Spirit of Truth" (Jn 16:13), the "Spirit of Grace" (Heb 10:29), the "Spirit of Glory" (1 Pet 4:14), the "Eternal Spirit" (Heb 9:14), the "Comforter" (Jn 15:26), and the list goes on.

Because the Holy Spirit is a person and not a 'force' it means that we have a relationship with him just as we do with the Father and the Son. In fact, it's the same relationship. This is important to understand, particularly when we discover what the Holy Spirit does.

THE WORK OF THE HOLY SPIRIT

Before I go any further there is one fact that must be made clear: the Holy Spirit lives inside every Christian. If you are not too familiar with Christianity this may seem very weird. "A spirit inside of me?" Not just 'a spirit' but the Holy Spirit. At the precise moment you trusted Jesus, you were given God's Spirit as a gift. (If you're in any doubt about this, have a look at Acts 2:38-39 and Romans 8:9.)

You may not have felt anything when you became a Christian but it is still true. Regardless of what you felt, or feel, if you are a Christian, God's Spirit is in you. This simple fact should be trusted and acted upon.

We read in 1 Corinthians 2:12:

We have...received...the Spirit who is from God, that we may understand what God has freely given us.

This sums up the work of the Holy Spirit inside a Christian. All the privileges and gifts from God are made real and available to the Christian because the Spirit makes it so. He brings God's life into the life of humans. An illustration may help.

Imagine trying to race a car around Bathurst's Mount Panorama race track. Some of us may do all right but unless you're an expert, it's a pretty difficult thing to do. However, suppose that Peter Brock, the world class racing driver, hopped in your car and took the wheel. Things would change, wouldn't they.

When God comes to live inside a Christian, it's sort of like Peter Brock taking the wheel. He makes us able to do things that would be impossible for us normally.

When we become Christians, God pours his Spirit into our hearts. He comes and sets up home in us. No longer are God and Christ something 'out there'–he is now living inside us!

I want to now explain some of the things the Spirit does in Christians.

HE GIVES LIFE

You may remember in Chapter 1, I explained that when someone becomes a Christian, they receive true life. What I didn't explain was that the source of this new life is the Holy Spirit himself. Before becoming a Christian, the Bible describes us as being 'dead' (remember the rose cut off from the rose bush?). This must change if we are to have a friendship with God and so the Holy Spirit actually enables you to come alive spiritually. The big word for this is 'regeneration' and it's sort of like putting new batteries into a Walkman or plugging a disconnected phone back into the socket.

HE HELPS US UNDERSTAND

Just as Satan is keen to deceive and lead Christians away from the truth, the Holy Spirit actively teaches and leads Christians into knowing the truth. He helps us realize that Jesus is Lord and that God is our Father and that we have a great future waiting for us in heaven (see 1 Cor 12:3; Rom 8:12-16; 2 Cor 5:5). He also makes us able to understand God better and better. As the Apostle Paul prayed for his Christian friends:

> **I keep asking that the God of our Lord Jesus Christ, the glorious Father, may give you the Spirit of wisdom and revelation, so that you may know him better.**
> **Ephesians 1:17**

As you read the Bible for yourself and hear good Bible teaching from others, the Author of the Bible himself, the Holy Spirit, will increase your knowledge of our wonderful God.

HE ENABLES US TO GROW IN OBEDIENCE

Before someone becomes a Christian, they are pretty much controlled by what the Bible calls the 'sinful nature'. This is the constant inward influence that causes you and me to live for ourselves and ignore God's guidelines. This, however, changes when we become Christians. Not that we stop sinning completely but we do receive a new nature. The Holy Spirit enables a Christian to obey God in a way otherwise impossible. Galatians 5:22-25 has a good list of the kinds of characteristics that God's Spirit can and will produce in us.

> **But the fruit of the Spirit is love, joy, peace, patience, kindness, goodness, faithfulness, gentleness and self-control. Against such things there is no law. Those who belong to Christ Jesus have crucified the sinful nature with its passions and desires. Since we live by the Spirit, let us keep in step with the Spirit.**

The Holy Spirit helps us to 'grow up' as Christians. He works in our lives to make us like Jesus.

HE CAN HELP US TO TELL OTHERS

The Holy Spirit can help us to tell others about Jesus. The Spirit wants to bring people's attention to Jesus and so he goes out of his way (actually it's right down his path) to accomplish that. He can give you boldness to speak about your faith and also makes your words have an effect on those you speak to–just like he did for the first Christians all those centuries ago:

> **And they were all filled with the Holy Spirit and spoke the word of God boldly.**   **Acts 4:31**

Telling others about Jesus without the Spirit's power is like going to war without weapons or, even worse, trying to play your stereo without electricity. So pray for people you're trying to talk to about Jesus. Ask God to work by his Spirit to help you say the right thing and to change the other person's heart.

HE HELPS US TO PRAY

Praying can sometimes be real hard going. Finding the desire, having the discipline or knowing what to pray, are just some of the things Christians struggle with in prayer. Let me be honest and say that prayer is sometimes just about the last thing I feel capable of. Sometimes my motivation is very low indeed, and I can't even think of *what* to pray let alone *how* to pray.

Being aware of our inability, God's Spirit helps us to pray.

> **In the same way, the Spirit helps us in our weakness. We do not know what we ought to pray for, but the Spirit himself intercedes for us with groans that words cannot express.**   **Romans 8:26**

I occasionally hear Christians ask, "What would Jesus do if he were here?" Now, that's a pretty good question if you're trying to work out how to behave in some tricky situation, but I can't help thinking to myself, "Well he is here, inside of us".

As Christians we have the enormous privilege of being indwelt by God himself. This is one of the most important things a Christian can know. Striving to live the Christian life on your own steam will very quickly grow tiresome. It will become boring and lack energy. However, if you daily trust and act upon the fact that the Holy Spirit lives in you, your life can and will be different. I'm not saying it will be a breeze but it will be full of energy–God's energy.

Check These Out

- ▶ 1 Cor 6:19
- ▶ Eph 4:29-32
- ▶ John 14:15-27
- ▶ John 16:5-16

BIBLE BASHING
How not to

A s WE PULLED OUT of Sydney for the eight-hour train trip to the Snowy Mountains, we were prepared. For weeks we had been discussing and praying together for that week in the middle of the Christmas holidays. As part of the preparation we took two types of bags–one for clothes, the other for the essential equipment of our mission. The latter we nicknamed the 'holy bag'. It was jam-packed full of Bibles, 'Jesus Saves' stickers and heaps of booklets explaining how to become a Christian.

It was the annual government camp held at the Snowy Mountains during the summer holidays. My friends and I had been to similar camps before, but at those we were more interested in picking fights and getting into girls' cabins than passing on Bibles and Christian booklets. This one was different. It was the year we had become Christians and we were keen to make use of this camp to pass on the message about Jesus. Within a few hours, our first bit of excitement began.

Luckily, we scored an eight-seater cabin on the train for ourselves. With our heads bowed, we began to pray for the week ahead, asking that if any chances to talk about Jesus came up, we would do a good job. One of the camp leaders passed by our cabin and curiously poked her head in. "What are you doing?" she asked suspiciously, undoubtedly thinking we were smoking a bong.

"We're praying", was our honest reply. Not at all convinced, she joined us to check things out.

So, we just kept on praying. Within a few minutes she was confused, but convinced, and left us with a vague, "That's nice, boys".

As usual, the first night of the camp was hyperactive and sleepless but bright and early the next morning, as everyone was rising, one of my friends announced that after lunch (during free time) there would be an open meeting to pray and talk about 'God and stuff'. Some of the guys in our cabin may have thought we were a bit strange but, sure enough, at free time, about fifteen of them turned up to see what was going on.

For over an hour, we chatted, asked and answered questions, and then concluded by praying. It was so successful we tried it the next day as well, and the next, and the next. In fact, we had some sort of Christian meeting on every day of the camp.

In addition to the meetings, we stuck the 'JESUS SAVES' stickers on almost every wall in the camp complex. I'm not sure that they had a huge effect, but it was another small way of raising people's awareness about Jesus.

One night after lights out, one of our group was busted for talking too loudly, too late at night. He was sent outside, along with another bloke who was busted for smoking, to stand under the stars for half an hour. As they stood there, staring up at the awesome starlit sky, the Christian turned to his fellow 'bustee' and said, "I know the guy who made all that". It was a strange way to start a conversation but it soon led to a great discussion of how we can get to know the God who made the universe. By the time the half hour of punishment was over, the other guy wanted to be a Christian.

This wasn't the only occasion like this either. By the end of the week, over ten guys and girls were keen to follow Jesus, the 'holy bag' was completely empty, and to top it off, two of our personal Bibles were stolen.

That camp taught us all a very valuable lesson: when you are unembarrassed, open and natural about your faith in Jesus, great things can happen. Watching the way my friends casually but enthusiastically included God in their conversations, convinced me that telling others about Jesus is not the awkward burden some Christians make it out to be, but an exciting privilege, and an opportunity to see God at work in peoples' lives.

That's what this chapter is about. It is just a few short pages describing the great privilege we have to pass on the news about our saviour.

WHY TELL OTHERS?

The first thing to realise about this topic is that we shouldn't feel guilt-bound to tell everyone we meet about Jesus. The Bible doesn't say that every Christian has to tell the gospel to every non-Christian they meet. It's not like the command to love people; there we have no choice—every Christian has to love everybody. But when it comes to passing on the news about Jesus there just isn't a big command. I've met too many Christians who feel guilty every time they hop off a bus having not shared their faith with the person sitting next to them. It should not be like this. This sort of pressure is unhealthy.

Having said this, the Bible does say we should, at least, be ready to *answer* for our faith when asked about it. Check out this passage for instance. The great Apostle Peter said:

> **Always be prepared to give an answer to everyone who asks you to give the reason for the hope that you have. But do this with gentleness and respect...**
> **1 Peter 3:15**

So, let me now give you a few reasons why being ready to pass on your faith in this way is important.

OUR LOVE FOR OTHERS

A couple of years ago, some mates and I went skiing. We love the sport but aren't exactly renowned for common sense on the slopes. One time, my friend, Ben, took off down the mountain in a moment of madness, straight towards a blind jump. The rest of us followed excitedly until we heard a desperate, "Don't do it!" from Ben. It turns out he'd had a 'near death encounter' with a tree stump just beyond the jump. We were very glad he had warned us.

Danger calls for warning, particularly when those at risk are people we care about. Warning others about God's judgement and telling them about the forgiveness and new life he offers is actually a way of expressing concern for the people we care about. It is not 'scare tactics' (and should never come across as such). It is simply being a good mate, like Ben on the ski slopes.

OUR LOVE FOR JESUS

The second good reason for telling others about Jesus is our love for him. He went through so much in order to take away the consequences of our disobedience. He was whipped, beaten and had a large wooden beam loaded on his blood-raw back. He was forced to carry it more than a kilometre to the place where they nailed spikes through his hands and feet. After hours of agony, he died. Jesus Christ, the mighty Creator, was murdered for the sake of you and me. Even though we were his enemies, he died to save us, to rescue us from our massive 'problem' (see Chapter 1).

Our God is so great, so loving, so gracious–surely those who love him will want others to give him the respect and love he deserves! The best way to get people to love and respect God is simply to tell them what he's done for them.

As we grow in our love for others and our love for Jesus, I'm sure we will also grow in our enthusiasm to let others know about our great God.

OK, let's assume that we are concerned for others and do love God, will this automatically make us effective in helping others know about Christ? Not necessarily. I think we also need to know *how* to tell others without being a 'Bible basher'.

HOW DO YOU TELL OTHERS?

Some time ago, I passed a bloke in the main street of Sydney who was preaching his heart out. He was shouting about Hell and reciting Bible verses at the poor unsuspecting shoppers. I felt quite embarrassed as I passed by, but decided to listen in on an argument that broke out between him and three other blokes who just happened to walking past.

As I listened in, it became clear these guys didn't have major problems with Christianity as such, but with the way the guy had been Bible-bashing them at full volume. I got to speak with these guys after the argument died down and my hunch was confirmed. These guys were actually quite interested in the Christian Faith, they just objected to the way it had been put across.

Situations like these have convinced me that there is a way *to*, and a way *not* to, explain the message of Jesus.

Here are four things that might help if you want to share your faith with those around you.

1. KNOW THE MESSAGE

Some Christians find it hard to know just what to say when the opportunity arises to talk about Jesus. Imagine going to a doctor who didn't know much about medicine. What good would they be to you?

Being confident of your topic is a great asset. If you are at all unclear of the Christian message, give Chapter 1 another read. Spend a bit of time working out what you would say (in your own words) if the chance came up.

2. LIVE THE MESSAGE

Lifestyle speaks louder than words. There is nothing worse than someone who says one thing and does another.

Jesus once said:

> **Your light must shine before people, so that they will see the good things you do and praise your Father in Heaven.** Matthew 5:16

If we are kind, honest, hard-working and reliable, people will notice. They'll be far more interested in our God than if we are selfish, dishonest, slack and unreliable.

Remember, though, don't just 'put on' these attributes. There's no point in faking it, because people see through that kind of act very easily.

As you strive to obey God, he'll give you the strength you need to live a life that brings him honour.

3. TELL THE MESSAGE

This does not mean 'Bible bashing'. Whenever there is an opportunity at school or work or uni, simply explain what you know. Jesus never shoved ideas down people's throats. He spoke lovingly, honestly, clearly and often simply answered questions. If we do the same, we will be a great benefit to those who want to hear.

A couple of years ago, I caught a taxi home from a hospital after visiting Elizabeth (now my wife) who was due for a very serious operation on the brain. I soon got talking to the driver about death and tragedies in general. He was very open to talk, but to be honest I felt tempted to leave the conversation without going any deeper. I had to decide whether or not I would talk about my faith and the hope it gives in the face of death.

All of us, from time to time, will get into conversations like this, where we will have to make a decision: "Will I mention my faith in Jesus, or won't I?" If we see these conversations as opportunities God has brought your way, it is often easier to take that exciting step, and say something about our great God.

4. USE 'GOD-TALK'

A book I recently read urged Christians to include God in their ordinary conversations with people. The writer described it as 'God-talk'. The more I've thought about it, and tried it, the more I'm convinced it is a very important way of passing your faith around. Let me give you a few examples of what I mean. Saying "God bless!" when you say good-bye to someone (or at the end of a letter/card) may seem like an old fashioned thing to do, but because it is so uncommon now-a-days, it stands out to people and might raise their awareness that at least some people still think God is involved in our lives. Or, suppose a friend shares some hard experience they're going through at the moment. Apart from offering any help you are able to give, you could also mention that you will remember to pray for them. Another example of 'God-talk' might be saying "God willing" when you're describing your career or travel plans to someone.

Of course, I'm not saying we should yell "Hallelujah" every five minutes–some religious words are plain unhelpful for non-Christians. All I am suggesting is that we mention God and our faith in him in our casual conversation. It's not going to change the world but will show the people around you that some people still think God is worth including in their lives.

5. PRAY

God hears prayer and is keen to give us our requests. He wants people to become Christians even more than you want them to become Christians.

There was a man named George Müller who lived last century. He was a very respected church minister who spent a lot of his time praying for others, that they would become Christians. By the time of his death, all but two people on his 'prayer list' had decided to follow Christ. Those last two became Christians some time after his funeral.

Now, not all of us can find the time and energy to pray as much as George Müller did, but we do have the same God and he is just as keen to answer our prayers. We should ask God to work in the hearts of the people we talk to, as well as for opportunities to share him with more people.

Some time ago I bumped into a girl who had been at the same summer camp my friends and I attended years before. I didn't remember her (we apparently didn't get to know each other at the camp) but she certainly remembered us. She especially remembered the way my friends had been so keen to let people know about Jesus. She even recalled the 'JESUS SAVES' stickers stuck all over the camp. It was great fun chatting with her, but more importantly, it was a great reminder to me that even the little things we do to try to pass on the message about Jesus can have a lasting influence on those around us.

MY BIGGEST MISTAKE
Living horizontally

I HAVE AN EMBARRASSING confession to make. For the first few years of my Christian life I was a total jerk. I'm serious! It took me at least five years as a follower of Jesus before I woke up to the biggest mistake of my Christian life.

So what was my mistake? Put simply, I thought the Christian life was all about loving God. That's right. I know it sounds weird, but that is a huge "oops", and heaps of us fall into the trap. Let me illustrate what I mean.

When I was about 16 and in my first Church youth group, I heard a talk that sounded great at the time, but, in fact was the last thing a jerk like me needed to hear. The talk explained that the Christian life was all about loving God with everything you've got. The speaker used an example that has stuck in my mind ever since. He said that in an orchestra, the musicians don't sit around trying to tune their instruments with each other–that would be chaos. What they do is tune individually to one perfectly tuned pitching fork or electronic tuner. That way, as long as they know they are in tune with the tuner, they will automatically be in tune with each other. This Christian speaker then concluded, "The Christian life is very similar. What we have to do is concentrate on loving God (that's being in tune) and all other relationships will be automatically in tune".

I sat there, as a 16 year-old Christian jerk, thinking, "Yeah! That makes heaps of sense". And off I went to live out what I learnt–loving God and letting all other relationships work themselves out. Let me show you what this sort of attitude ends up looking like.

When I was about 17, I was in my room one Saturday morning reading the Bible and praying. I heard mum call out from the other end of the house, "Johhhhn, can you please rake the leaves in the front garden!"

I was in the middle of some pretty serious praying, so I called back, "Not just now mum, I'm really busy".

A few minutes later I heard mum yell, "Will you rake the leaves … now!"

I again called back, "I'll do it later. I am really busy".

Within seconds, mum was in my room, and I was busted. After she walked out I felt quite pleased with myself. After all, I was putting God first in my life. Surely, praying and reading the Bible is more important than raking the leaves. Getting into trouble made me feel even better about it all. I thought that I was being persecuted for loving God so much. But I wasn't. I was persecuted for being a jerk.

It never dawned on me that God would rather I showed love to my mum than spend the time praying. (Actually, I could easily have prayed while raking the leaves anyhow.)

I am sure you see my point. The Christian life is not all about loving

God. It is all about loving God and loving people. Let me prove it.

When a teacher came up to Jesus (Matt 22:34-40) and said, "Teacher, which is the greatest commandment?", how did Jesus answer? He said, "Love God with all your heart …and the second is like it…" Now, the strange thing about this is that the teacher didn't ask for a second one. He asked which was the "greatest commandment"–singular, not plural. But Jesus didn't believe in just ONE command, but TWO: "Love God with all your heart…and the second is like it: love your neighbour as your-self".

Decades later when the Apostle John was writing his letter, he must have recalled the words his Lord had spoken, because what he says in chapter 4 is almost identical:

> **If anyone says, "I love God", yet hates his brother, he is a liar. For anyone who does not love his brother, whom he has seen, cannot love God, whom he has not seen. And he has given us this command: whoever loves God must also love his brother.**　　　　　**1 John 4:20-21**

This is a tough call. Unless I love the people around me–my mum, brothers, wife, friends, non-friends, etc–I am not allowed to say, "I love God". There is no way around this. I could be the most (seemingly) passionate Christian–someone who always spends time praying, and reading the Bible; someone who is constantly on the lookout to tell people about Jesus; someone who sings at church with great enthusiasm. But if I do not show keen and practical love to the people around me, I am a liar. All my apparently 'passionate' spiritual activities are false, a sham, a lie. That is what the Apostle John says, and he got it straight from the horse's mouth.

I can't even take credit for waking up to this reality. It was my broth-er who pointed these truths out to me. I had been a Christian for five or six years, and was singing and speaking in a full-time Christian band. I was so busy serving God in my band's ministry that I had forgotten about many of my family and friendship responsibilities back in Sydney. Some of my closest friends had needs that I should have tried to help with. But I was off 'saving the world', doing my thing for God, I thought. Then I got a letter from my brother. Actually, it was more like a semi-trailer than a piece of paper. In it, he pointed out to me that being a Christian is not all about loving God. It is all about loving God and people. He reminded me of some verses in the Bible–verses I had read a million times but had never put into practice; verses very much like those I just quoted, that forced me to face up to the fact that I am not allowed to say I love God if I don't also love people.

So there it is. There's my embarrassing confession. I wish I had learnt the lesson earlier, but at least it can serve as a warning. Don't be a jerk. Don't fall into the trap of thinking the Christian life is all about loving God. Be like Jesus. His love for God expressed itself as love for us. His death on the cross is the obvious example. In fact, the cross is not only a good example, it's a good picture and reminder of the whole Christian life–a vertical axis to remind us to love God and a horizontal axis to remind us to love people.

HANGING IN THERE
The key to remaining a Christian

"Not very close to God…"
"Pretty slack spiritually…I just don't seem to do anything about it."
"God's not in my life terribly much…"

THESE COMMENTS ARE taken from the diary I kept a number of years ago. It pretty clearly describes how I felt about life and God during that time.

From age 15 to 17 I guess you could say I was a very 'full-on' Christian. Shortly after this, though, things started to go wrong. For about the next two years, I dragged my faith down into compromise after compromise and tried hard to forget about God.

I always felt awkward about this disobedience, however. I couldn't get drunk without feeling guilty and never felt comfortable with certain relationships I became involved in. I stopped going to church regularly, but every now and then I dared to slip in late and sit up the back where no-one could see me. For most of the service, I'd have this sick feeling inside my stomach, knowing how much of a hypocrite I was. As soon as it finished, I made a quick exit, making sure no Christians had a chance to 'get me' and ask how I was going.

For me, Christianity had become 'boring'. Praying was a drag, the Bible seemed dead and Christians got on my nerves. I still believed it all; I just couldn't imagine myself ever getting committed to God again.

My disobedient lifestyle eventually backfired and I found myself calling out to God for help. I said something like, "Please Lord, get me out of this situation. I promise to come back to you".

To cut a long story short, things did work out. God used a set of circumstances to bring me back to himself. Boy, did I come back! I returned to church regularly, no longer avoided Christians and loved reading the Bible again. Even though I had pushed God aside for so long, he forgave me. I had left him but he had never left me. I had ignored him but he still loved me. I had disobeyed him but he was faithful and didn't condemn me. That's pretty fantastic!

For the next six months or so, I sailed along quite happily, unaware that I was sailing right into more hassles of a very different kind.

In my renewed enthusiasm, I tried to make up for lost time. I prayed heaps (a couple of hours each day) and read the Bible in most of my spare time. To everyone around, I must have appeared a kind of 'super Christian', but inside I was driven by a sort of guilt. I felt I needed to keep God happy with me in order to remain a Christian. Instead of trusting in God's mercy, I trusted in my own ability to keep God pleased. This was a major, major mistake.

To make things worse, I had a lot of doubts to grapple with as well. Whenever I doubted something about God, I felt guilty and wondered whether I was really a Christian or not. This only led me to try harder at being a 'super Christian'. Finally, I was worn out, fed up and didn't know what to do.

If this is depressing you, stay tuned because it was at this point that I learnt the most important lesson of my Christian life.

It's taken me about two hours to think of how to summarise this lesson into one sentence, but here it is:

God is happy with his children.

I know this sounds simple but the implications of it are huge. I discovered from the Bible that I could not become a better or more stable Christian, by my own effort. God is pleased with me because Christ took all my guilt on himself. It has nothing to do with how much I pray, or how often I tell others about Jesus. Even when I disobey him, God does not think to himself, "You bad Christian. How dare you disobey me?" As it says in Romans 8:1:

Therefore, there is now no condemnation for those who are in Christ Jesus.

Think of the person you love most in your life. If they wrong you in some way, sure you get upset, even cross–but you still love them and value that relationship. This is similar to God's attitude toward Christians, except that he is infinitely more loving than you or me.

The LORD is compassionate and gracious, slow to anger, abounding in love...he does not treat us as our sins deserve or repay us according to our iniquities. For as high as the heavens are above the earth, so great is his love for those who fear him; as far as the east is from the west, so far has he removed our transgressions from us. As a father has compassion on his children, so the LORD has compassion on those who fear him.

Psalm 103:8-13

Reading the Bible, praying, and obeying Jesus–these are all important aspects of life. It matters very much to God how we live. However, if our motivation to do these things is guilt and trying to earn God's favour, then we'll end up pretty frustrated. On the other hand, if our motivation is gratitude, and our strength comes from God's Spirit, we will be anything but frustrated. We have to keep reminding ourselves: God is happy with his children.

The man in the drawing on the front cover didn't need to try so hard to carry all the burdens of life because God was there to support him. He will support us also. Put simply, the key to 'hanging in there' as a Christian is to know that you are being 'held' by a God who, because of Jesus, is very happy with you.

To him [God] who is able to keep you from falling and to present you before his glorious presence without fault and with great joy...   Jude 1:24

I wanted to end this book on a fairly personal note and show that being a Christian has been a struggle for me. The person who said that "Christianity is a bed of roses", forgot to mention the thorns. Living for God is often hard going. Handling occasional insults, trusting in Someone we can't see and living in a world that doesn't like Jesus–these are things that don't come naturally to us humans. Remember, though: God is happy with his children. He will always provide us with what we need to become stable, devoted followers of Jesus.

So, hang in there! And have fun doing it.

God bless you heaps,

John.

APPENDIX

Promises, promises

WHAT FOLLOWS IS A list of some of God's best promises, as found in the Bible. Some of them may not relate directly to your life right now but you can always come back to them as the need arises.

Someone once said, "Christianity is not necessarily a way around life's problems but a way straight through them". If we can learn to take God at his word, regardless of how we feel or the circumstances around us, we will discover one of the most important lessons in the Christian life.

God is trustworthy. So are all his promises.

Christians are a bit like spiritual millionaires and their cash is God's promises. Some Christians aren't aware of his many promises and so live more like beggars than millionaires. This is a bit sad. Imagine how you would feel giving your best friend a million bucks which they never spent, going around sad and living in rags. This is a bit like how God feels when his children don't trust his promises and go through life unsure of his love, forgiveness and protection.

If you're a Christian, you are a millionaire–go spend it!

WHEN YOU FEEL ALONE

You hem me in–behind and before;
you have laid your hand on me...
Where can I go from your Spirit?
Where can I flee from your presence?
If I go up to the heavens, you are there;
If I make my bed in the depths you are there.
If I rise on the wings of the dawn,
if I settle on the far side of the sea,
even there your hand will guide,
your right hand will hold me fast.   Psalm 139:5,7-10

I will be with you always, to the very end of the age.
Matthew 28:20

WHEN AFRAID

When I am afraid,
I will trust you.
In God, whose word I praise,
in God I trust; I will not be afraid.
What can mortal man do to me?   Psalm 56:3-4

Be strong and courageous. Do not be afraid or terrified because of them, for the Lord your God goes with you; he will never leave you; he will never forsake you.   Deuteronomy 31:6

WHEN FEELING GUILTY

If we confess our sins, he is faithful and just and will forgive us our sins and purify us from all unrighteousness.   1 John 1:8-9

Therefore, there is now no condemnation for those who are in Christ Jesus. Romans 8:1

As far as the east is from the west, so far has he removed our transgressions from us.   Psalm 103:12

WHEN STRESSED OUT

Do not be anxious about anything, but in everything, by prayer and petition, with thanksgiving, present your requests to God. And the peace of God, which transcends all understanding, will guard your hearts and minds in Christ Jesus.   Philippians 4:6-7

WHEN DEPRESSED

We know that in all things God works for the good of those who love him.
                                        Romans 8:28

I remember my affliction and my wandering,
the bitterness and the gall.
I well remember them,
and my soul is downcast within me.
Yet this I call to mind and therefore I have hope:
Because of the Lord's great love we are not consumed,
for his compassions never fail.
They are new every morning;
great is your faithfulness.
I say to myself, "The Lord is my portion;
therefore I will wait for him".
The Lord is good to those whose hope is in him,
to the one who seeks him;
it is good to wait quietly for the salvation of the Lord.
                                Lamentations 3:19-26

For his anger lasts only a moment, but his favour lasts a lifetime; weeping may remain for a night, but rejoicing comes in the morning.

Psalm 30:5

WHEN ANGRY

In your anger do not sin. Do not let the sun go down while you are still angry.

Ephesians 4:26

WHEN NEEDING GUIDANCE

Blessed are those whose ways are blameless,
who walk according to the law of the Lord.
Blessed are they who keep his statutes
and seek him with all their heart.
They do nothing wrong;
they walk in his ways...
How can a young man keep his way pure?
By living according to your word.

Psalm 119:1-3,9

If any of you lacks wisdom, he should ask God, who gives generously to all without finding fault, and it will be given him.

James 1:5

PROMISES IN PRAYER

So I say to you: Ask and it will be given to you: seek and you will find; knock and the door will be opened to you... If you, then, who are evil, know how to give good gifts to your children, how much more will your Father in heaven give good gifts to those who ask him!

Matthew 7:7,11

WHEN TEMPTED TO SIN

Because he [Jesus] himself suffered when he was tempted, he is able to help those who are being tempted.   Hebrews 2:18

Submit yourselves, then, to God. Resist the devil, and he will flee from you.

James 4:7

For we know that our old self was crucified with him so that the body of sin might be rendered powerless, that we should no longer be slaves to sin...

Romans 6:6

GOD'S LOVE

For as high as the heavens are above the earth, so great is his love for those who fear [or highly respect] him.   Psalm 103:11

For I am convinced that neither death nor life, neither angels nor demons, neither the present nor the future, nor any powers, neither height nor depth, nor anything else in all creation, will be able to separate us from the love of God that is in Christ Jesus our Lord.

Romans 8:38-39

GOD'S FORGIVENESS

If we confess our sins, he is faithful and just and will forgive us our sins and purify us from all unrighteousness.   1 John 1:9

In him we have redemption through his blood, the forgiveness or sins...

Ephesians 1:7

You are kind and forgiving, O Lord, abounding in love to all who call to you.

Psalm 86:5

OUR ETERNAL LIFE

Whoever believes in the Son [of God] has eternal life...

John 3:36

...the gift of God is eternal life in Christ Jesus our Lord.

Romans 6:23

GOD'S POWER

Say to God, "How awesome are your deeds! So great is your power that your enemies cringe before you. All the earth bows down to you; they sing praise to you..."   Psalm 66:3-4

For nothing is impossible for God.   Luke 1:37

GOD'S PROTECTION

You are my hiding place; you will protect me from trouble and surround me with songs of deliverance.   Psalm 32:7

GOD'S KNOWLEDGE

He determines the number of the stars and calls them each by name. Great is our Lord...his understanding has no limit.
                                                                Psalm 147:4-5

For you created my inmost being;
you knit me together in my mother's womb.
I praise you because I am fearfully and wonderfully made;
your works are wonderful,
I know that full well.   Psalm 139:13-14

VICTORY OVER THE DEVIL

The reason the Son of God appeared was to destroy the Devil's work.
                                                                1 John 3:8

GOD'S PROMISES

Let us hold unswervingly to the hope we profess, for he [God] who promised is faithful.   Hebrews 10:23

Other books by John Dickson...

A Hell of a Life
(From Manger to Megastar)

John Dickson's latest evangelistic book for young people is already establishing itself as another classic. The usual Dickson trademarks are all there—clarity, simplicity, an engaging style, and a very firm grasp of the issues.

A Hell of a Life focuses on Jesus—his life, his death and resurrection, his supreme and abiding relevance for everyone. Ideal age range: 18-30.

"This book is called *A Hell of a Life* for two reasons. Firstly, because Jesus' life was so incredible. It was a life full of action, danger, mystery and power. But there is a more unusual and serious reason for the title. According to Jesus himself, the focus of his whole life's work was to die for you and me...Put simply, he took Hell for us so that we wouldn't have to."
(quote from Chapter 13) 128 pages

A Sneaking Suspicion
(with Study Guide)

This enormously popular book by John Dickson has proved to be a great tool in sharing the gospel, especially with younger people (15-25 years).

A Sneaking Suspicion talks about things that matter—things like life, death, relationships, sex, suffering, meaning, and God—things that are important but that we don't often talk about.

Great, readable advice about life and eternal life. 128 pages

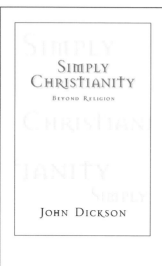

Simply Christianity: Beyond Religion

In the tradition of *A Sneaking Suspicion* and *A Hell of a Life* comes John Dickson's *Simply Christianity: Beyond Religion*. Based on the enquirers' course of the same name, *Simply Christianity: Beyond Religion* is written for a general adult readership, and promises to become a standard way to introduce our friends and family to the core message of Christianity—that Jesus is God's Christ, the ruler of the world, who came to rescue us through his death, so that all might be able to repent and find forgiveness in him.

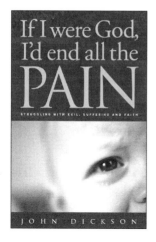

If I were God, I'd end all the pain

Why doesn't God do something about all the pain and suffering? Why does he let it happen? In fact, can we still believe in God in the face of all the evil in the world?

In the first of a new series of short apologetic books, John Dickson looks honestly at these questions, and provides some compelling biblical answers. He looks briefly at the alternative explanations for suffering provided by Hinduism, Buddhism, Islam and Atheism, shows why the perspective of the Bible is the best one available, and points finally to Christ's death and the gospel of mercy as God's answer to our suffering world.

If I were God, I'd end all the pain is a superb book to give to a non-Christian person. It deals with one of the most often-asked questions in an honest, sensitive and convincing way. It will no doubt prove just as useful for Christians who want a simple, satisfying answer to this perennial question.

About Matthias Media

Ever since 'St Matthias Press and Tapes' first opened its doors in 1988, under the auspices of St Matthias Anglican Church, Centennial Park, in Sydney, our aim has been to provide the Christian community with products of a uniformly high standard—both in their biblical faithfulness and in the quality of the writing and production.

Now known as Matthias Media, we have grown to become a nationwide provider of user-friendly resources for ministry, with Christians of all sorts using our Bible studies, books, Briefings, audio cassettes, videos, training courses—you name it.

For more information about the range of Matthias Media resources, call us on Freecall 1800 814 360 (or in Sydney 9663-1478), or fax us on (02) 9663-3265, and we will send you a free catalogue. Or you can e-mail us at sales@matthiasmedia.com.au. Or visit our Web site at: **www.matthiasmedia.com.au**

Buy direct from us and save

If you order your Matthias Media resources direct from us, you not only save time and money, you invest in more great resources for the future:

- you save time—we usually despatch our orders within 24 hours of receiving them

- you save money—our normal prices are better than other retailers' prices (plus if you order in bulk, you'll save even more)

- you help keep us afloat—because we get more from each sale, buying from us direct helps us to stay alive in the difficult world of publishing.